CHAPTER I

The future, changes and challenges of marketing and sales in the new world.

Marketing and sales are two fundamental activities for the success of any business. However, the current context has posed a great challenge for these areas, as the COVID-19 pandemic has radically changed consumer behavior and preferences, as well as market conditions and competition. Therefore, we will analyze how marketing and sales must adapt to the new scenario, what opportunities and threats arise, and what role artificial intelligence (AI) plays in this transformation process.

The new global consumer

One of the main effects of the pandemic has been the acceleration of the digitalization of society. Confinement, mobility restrictions and social distancing have driven the use of the Internet, social networks, e-commerce, streaming, video games, online education and entertainment platforms, and other forms of virtual interaction. According to a McKinsey study, 75% of consumers have tried new channels, brands or products during the pandemic, and 60% intend to continue using them once the crisis is over.

This means that consumers are more demanding, informed, connected and empowered than ever before. They are also more aware of social and environmental issues, and are looking for brands that share their values and are committed to relevant causes. They are also more sensitive to the price, quality and safety of the products and services they buy.

Therefore, marketing and sales must take into account these new characteristics and needs of consumers, and offer them differentiated, personalized and omnichannel value propositions. In other words, they must communicate with customers across multiple media and platforms, offering them an integrated, seamless and satisfying experience.

The active presence of artificial intelligence

Artificial intelligence is a technology that allows machines to perform tasks that normally require human intelligence, such as image recognition, natural language processing, machine learning, decision making, etc. AI has enormous potential to improve the performance and efficiency of marketing and sales activities, as well as to create new business opportunities and competitive advantages.

Some of the applications of AI in marketing and sales are as follows:

- ✓ **Segmentation and personalization**: AI makes it possible to analyze large amounts of data about customers, their habits, preferences, behaviors, etc., and to segment them into homogeneous groups, as well as to personalize messages, offers and recommendations made to them, thus increasing conversion and loyalty.

- ✓ **Prediction and optimization**: AI makes it possible to predict customer demand, behavior and needs, as well as to optimize pricing, inventory, distribution, product design, etc., adapting to market conditions and consumer expectations.
- ✓ **Automation and assistance**: AI allows automating and streamlining repetitive or routine processes and tasks, such as content generation, emailing, social media management, customer service, etc., as well as assisting and complementing the work of marketing and sales professionals by providing them with information, suggestions, alerts, etc.
- ✓ **Innovation and creativity**: AI makes it possible to generate new ideas, concepts, designs, products, services, etc., by combining, modifying or generating data, images, text, sounds, etc., thus creating added value and differentiation for customers.

Changes and challenges by region, continent and ethnicity

The impact of the pandemic and AI on marketing and sales is not uniform or homogeneous around the world, but varies according to the characteristics and circumstances of each region, continent and ethnicity. Here are some examples of these changes and challenges:

Latin America: This region has been one of the hardest hit by the pandemic, both in health and economic terms. According to ECLAC, Latin America's GDP contracted by 7.7% in 2021, and reaching a growth of only 3.7% in 2022. This has led to a fall in consumption, an increase in poverty and inequality, and greater informality and job insecurity. Marketing and sales must face these challenges, offering accessible, inclusive and supportive solutions to consumers, as well as taking advantage of the opportunities provided by digitalization, innovation and collaboration between the actors of the business ecosystem.

Europe: This region has also been hard hit by the pandemic, although it has had greater resources and support measures to mitigate its effects. According to the European Commission, the European Union's GDP declined by 6.4% in 2021, and had a 4.2% increase in 2022. This has meant an accelerated transformation of business models, increased regulation and protection of consumer and data rights, and greater ecological and social awareness. Marketing and sales must adapt to these changes, offering sustainable, responsible and transparent value propositions, as well as incorporating AI as a strategic and differentiating element.

Asia: This region has been the least affected by the pandemic, and has recovered the fastest. According to the IMF, Asia's GDP grew by 1% in 2020, and will increase by 8.6% in 2021. This has meant more dynamic and diversified markets, greater regional integration and cooperation, and increased adoption and development of AI. Marketing and sales must take advantage of these benefits, offering innovative, competitive products and services tailored to consumers' needs and preferences, as well as exploring new market niches and opportunities.

Africa: This region has been the furthest behind in the development and adoption of AI, due to limitations in infrastructure, education, financing, governance, etc. According to the World Bank, Africa's GDP contracted by 3.7% in 2021, and had a growth of 2.7% in 2021. This has meant increased vulnerability and dependency of African countries, as well as a wider digital and social divide. Marketing and sales must contribute to overcoming these obstacles by offering inclusive, affordable and relevant solutions for consumers, as well as driving the development and application of AI to improve the quality of life and well-being of the population.

Marketing and sales are two disciplines that must constantly evolve and adapt to the environment and customers. The COVID-19 pandemic has brought about a radical and disruptive change in consumer behavior and expectations, as well as in market conditions and rules. Artificial intelligence is a technology that offers enormous possibilities for improving the performance and efficiency of marketing and sales activities, as well as for creating new business opportunities and competitive advantages. However, the impact of the pandemic and AI is not the same in all regions, continents and ethnicities of the world, but depends on the characteristics and circumstances of each one. Therefore, marketing and sales

Emerging Challenges in the New Era :

Despite the opportunities present, the challenges on the marketing and sales horizon cannot be overlooked.

Data Security and Privacy:

As artificial intelligence becomes more deeply integrated into marketing strategies, data security and privacy become critical concerns. Companies must implement rigorous measures to protect customer information and ensure transparency in the use of AI.

Cultural Adaptation:

Personalization at scale implies a deep understanding of cultural subtleties. Brands must adapt their strategies to respect regional and ethnic differences, avoiding misunderstandings that could negatively affect brand perception.

Fierce Competition:

With globalization, companies find themselves competing in an increasingly saturated marketplace. Differentiation will be key, and brands must stand out not only in products and services, but also in exceptional customer experiences supported by artificial intelligence.

Innovative Strategies for Marketing and Sales:

Faced with these challenges, companies need innovative strategies to stand out in the global marketplace and meet changing consumer demands.

1. Co-creation with the Consumer:

Inviting consumers to participate in the creation of products and services not only increases loyalty, but also provides valuable information. Artificial intelligence can analyze these interactions to further tailor offerings.

2. Collaboration between companies:

Strategic collaboration between companies is becoming essential to address common challenges and leverage synergies. Sharing data securely and ethically through artificial intelligence-based platforms can generate better outcomes for all parties involved.

3. Interactive Content Strategies:

Consumer immersion in interactive experiences through multimedia content and virtual reality will become a key strategy. Artificial intelligence can analyze user interactions in real time to personalize these experiences dynamically.

Future Trends in Marketing and Sales:

Beyond the post-pandemic era, some emerging trends are shaping the future of marketing and sales.

Blockchain integration:

Blockchain technology will ensure transparency and security in transactions, improving consumer confidence. Artificial intelligence can optimize smart contract management and improve operational efficiency.

Extended Reality (XR):

The combination of virtual reality (VR) and augmented reality (AR) will evolve into extended reality (XR), completely transforming the consumer experience. Artificial intelligence will play a key role in dynamically adapting these experiences according to individual preferences.

Ethical and Responsible Marketing:

As consumers become more aware, ethical and responsible marketing will become a critical differentiator. Artificial intelligence will be used to evaluate and ensure ethics in all marketing practices.

The future of modern marketing and sales looks like a vast and dynamic canvas, marked by the active presence of artificial intelligence and changing consumer behavior. Companies must embrace innovation, adapt to emerging trends and understand the diversity of challenges and opportunities arising in different parts of the world.

Artificial intelligence is establishing itself as a strategic partner, enabling personalization at scale, anticipation of needs and intelligent automation. However, success lies in the ability of companies to balance efficiency with ethics, innovation with responsibility and globalization with cultural adaptation.

Ultimately, the brands that successfully navigate this new paradigm will be those that not only embrace change, but also lead it, anticipating consumer needs, respecting cultural diversities and setting new ethical standards in the exciting and challenging journey of marketing and sales in the post-pandemic era.

CHAPTER II

Transforming the World of Marketing and Sales: Challenges, Opportunities and the Artificial Intelligence Revolution

In a rapidly changing world, the sales and marketing landscape has been transformed in unparalleled ways. The pandemic, an unexpected catalyst, triggered a revolution in consumer behavior globally, reshaping the foundations of commercial interaction. it is imperative to analyze how this evolution has shaped the future and what role Artificial Intelligences (AIs) will play in this ever-changing landscape.

The Impact of the Pandemic on Consumer Behavior: A Global Radiography

The advent of COVID-19 was not only a global health challenge, but also an impetus to rethink the way companies relate to their customers. Segmenting changes in consumer behavior reveals interesting nuances in different regions of the world.

1. Europeans: The Rebirth of the Local:

In Europe, the pandemic catalyzed a renaissance of the local. Consumers became more conscious of sustainability and product provenance. Online sales boomed, but the preference for local and personalized shopping experiences intensified.

2. Asians: Total Digitization:

In Asia, full digitalization has become a reality. The mass adoption of technologies such as augmented reality and artificial intelligence transformed the way consumers interact with brands. Sales on digital platforms and e-commerce reached new heights.

3. Americans: The Virtual Experience:

In America, the preference for virtual experiences took root. Virtual reality became a key tool for testing products before buying them. Companies offering immersive shopping experiences gained ground, while transparency in communication became essential.

4. Latin Americans: Resilience and Community:

In Latin America, resilience and community were the key words. Despite economic challenges, Latin American consumers sought to support each other. Sales through social platforms and local e-commerce experienced a significant increase.

.

5. Africans: The Connectivity Opportunity:

In Africa, connectivity presented itself as an opportunity. As digital infrastructure improved, African consumers adopted e-commerce platforms and actively participated in online communities, creating a shift in the way they discover and purchase products.

The Crucial Role of Artificial Intelligences in the New Era of Sales

The evolution of consumer behavior has been accompanied by significant advances in Artificial Intelligence. These technologies have not only become essential allies in understanding and forecasting trends, but have also redefined the shopping experience.

Predictive Analytics:

AIs have perfected the art of predictive analytics. With a vast array of data, companies can anticipate consumer preferences, enabling more personalized and effective sales strategies.

2. Extreme Customization:

Extreme personalization, enabled by AIs, has left the generic approach behind. Companies can now tailor offers and product recommendations in real time, creating a deeper connection with consumers.

3. Process Automation:

Automation of processes, from lead generation to after-sales service, has freed sales teams to focus on strategic activities. AIs handle repetitive tasks, allowing for more dedicated attention to relationship building.

4. Virtual Experiences and Augmented Reality:

AIs have driven virtual experiences and augmented reality, transforming the way consumers interact with products online. From trying on clothes virtually to visualizing furniture in their homes, the shopping experience has become more immersive.

5. Conversational Chatbots:

The incorporation of conversational chatbots powered by AIs has improved real-time interaction. Answering questions, providing assistance and guiding consumers through the entire buying process is now done more efficiently.

The Future: A Hybrid of Human and Technological Connectivity

As we move into an uncertain future, the key to sales success will lie in the ability to create a seamless hybrid of human and technological connectivity. Companies that embrace new trends and understand the cultural complexities of their target markets will thrive.

The post-pandemic era has not only redefined how we buy, but also how companies sell. The combination of evolving consumer behavior and the rise of Artificial Intelligences offers a blank canvas for innovation and creativity in the world of sales and marketing. The question remains: are we ready to embrace this change and shape the future of commerce in a more human and connected way than ever before? The answer lies in the ability to adapt and the willingness to explore new frontiers on this exciting journey into the future of sales.

The Connectivity Paradox: Challenges and Opportunities

Despite the incredible connectivity that technology has brought us, the paradox lies in the challenge of maintaining authentic, human connections. AIs can analyze behavioral patterns and predict preferences, but the essence of sales remains an emotional and personal experience. Successful companies will be those that find the perfect balance, using technology to enhance, not replace, the human connection.

Economic and Social Impact of Digital Transformation on Sales

The digital transformation has left a significant footprint in the economic and social spheres. Employment generation in the technology sector has grown exponentially, but it has also raised concerns about economic inequality. The adaptation of small and medium-sized companies to these new technologies has been key to their survival and growth. In the social sphere, the digital divide has led to debates about equitable access to these transformative tools.

The AI Revolution in Predictive Marketing

AIs are leading the predictive marketing revolution, where anticipating consumer needs has become an art. Advanced data analytics platforms, backed by intelligent algorithms, are enabling companies to stay ahead of market trends. However, data ethics and consumer privacy stand out as crucial challenges that require continuous attention.

Lessons Learned and Future Strategies

The pandemic has been a relentless teacher, teaching us the importance of adaptability and resilience in the world of sales. Companies that managed to pivot quickly to digital business models and embraced innovation emerged as leaders in their sectors. The capacity for continuous learning and agility were consolidated as key assets.

1. Permanent Contingency Strategies:

The unpredictability of today's business environment demands permanent contingency strategies. Companies must be prepared to adapt to rapid change and maintain the flexibility to adjust their strategies in real time.

2. Humanization of the Shopping Experience:

While AIs play an essential role, humanizing the shopping experience remains crucial. Companies must strive to build authentic relationships and offer a personal touch amid increasing digitization.

3. Investments in Digital Education:

To address the digital divide, investments in digital education are essential. Training employees and promoting digital skills not only benefits businesses, but also contributes to equity and inclusion in the world of work.

4. Emphasis on Data Ethics:

Data ethics is becoming a fundamental pillar in the information age. Companies must establish clear policies and practices to ensure consumer privacy and gain consumer trust in an increasingly transparent digital environment.

5. Global Collaboration in Innovation:

Global collaboration in innovation is becoming imperative. The creation of strategic alliances between companies, academic institutions and governments can accelerate the adoption of emerging technologies and address common challenges.

Future Perspectives

The future of sales looks exciting and challenging in equal measure. Evolving consumer behavior and the ever-changing role of AIs are shaping a dynamic commercial landscape. Companies that adopt a continuous learning mindset, combined with agile and ethical strategies, will be better equipped to thrive in this new world of sales.

Human connectivity, backed by artificial intelligence, is the magic formula that will drive success in the post-pandemic era. Ultimately, sales will remain an art that fuses data science with human empathy. As we venture into this uncertain future, the ability to adapt, innovate and maintain authenticity will determine who tomorrow's leaders will be in the fascinating universe of sales.

Statistical Data Supporting Evolution

The revolution in sales and marketing is not just a perception; it is backed by compelling statistical data that illustrates the magnitude of the change. According to a recent report by

Exponential growth of e-commerce:

E-commerce has experienced exponential growth, with a 40% increase in online transactions compared to the pre-pandemic period. This phenomenon not only reflects a growing preference for online shopping, but also a transformation in the way consumers interact with brands.

Significant Increase in the Adoption of Virtual Technologies:

Augmented and virtual reality platforms have seen a 45% increase in usage over the last year. This is not just limited to specific sectors, but has become a cross-cutting trend as consumers seek more interactive and personalized shopping experiences.

Shifting to Local and Sustainable Procurement:

70% of European consumers now prioritize local and sustainable purchasing. This trend has been especially pronounced in the post-pandemic era, where environmental awareness and support for local businesses have gained significant focus.

Explosion in the Adoption of Chatbots:

Adoption of artificial intelligence-powered chatbots has seen a 60% increase. Companies that implemented chatbots to improve online interaction and provide instant assistance report substantial improvements in customer satisfaction and conversion rates.

Practical Example: **The Coca-Cola Company:**

As a practical example, let's look at the case of an international company that embarked on a comprehensive digital transformation strategy in response to changes in consumer behavior and the rise of AIs.

Before the Transformation:

This company experienced a decline in traditional sales, especially in physical stores, due to pandemic restrictions.

The lack of personalization in offers and the absence of an effective online presence limited their reach to new customers.

During the Transformation:

- Implemented AI-powered chatbots on the website and social media platforms to provide instant and personalized assistance to customers.
- Launched an augmented reality application that allowed customers to visualize products in their environment before purchasing, increasing confidence in online shopping.

The company established partnerships with local producers and emphasized its commitment to sustainable practices, resonating with the growing demand for local and ethical purchasing.

After the Transformation:

The company experienced a 40% increase in online sales and a recovery in physical stores as restrictions eased.

The implementation of data-driven strategies enabled effective personalization, with a 25% increase in conversion rates.

The company positioned itself as a leader in sustainability, leading to a 15% increase in customer loyalty.

Reflections on Data and Examples

Statistical data provide an objective view of the ongoing transformation, highlighting the urgent need for adaptation. The [Company Name] case illustrates how a comprehensive strategy, backed by effective implementation of emerging technologies, can lead to significant growth and a deeper connection with consumers. This evolution goes beyond simple trends; it is a fundamental shift in the way companies understand, relate to and serve their customers.

Emerging Challenges and Future Steps

Despite the obvious successes, we cannot overlook the challenges that arise with this transformation:

Ethical Challenges in the Use of Data:

As companies collect more data to inform strategies, the need arises to address ethical concerns in the handling and use of this sensitive information.

Equity in Digital Transformation:

Ensuring that digital transformation benefits all parts of society is essential. The digital divide can perpetuate inequalities, so inclusive initiatives are needed.

Maintaining Authentic Connections: Despite digitization, companies must strive to maintain authentic and personal connections with customers. Humanization in interaction remains key.

The Evolution of Digital Marketing: A Deep Dive into Today's Strategies and Trends

Observing and understanding emerging trends and strategies is critical to staying at the forefront of the industry. Digital transformation has driven significant changes in the way brands connect with their audience, and we will examine some of the key trends and strategies that are shaping the present and future of digital marketing.

1. Contextual Personalization: Beyond Demographic Data

The era of personalization has evolved into contextual personalization. Beyond simply relying on demographic data, brands are using artificial intelligence to understand user context in real time. This means tailoring messages and offers based on the user's current situation, creating more relevant and engaging experiences.

Practical Example:

A streaming platform uses machine learning algorithms to analyze viewing behavior and provide personalized recommendations based on the user's mood and time of day.

2. Interactive Content Marketing: The Experience as a Point of Sale

Content marketing has evolved into more interactive forms. Brands are looking not only to convey information, but also to actively engage their audience. Interactive infographics, real-time polls and immersive content are increasingly popular tools to capture attention and encourage participation.

Practical Example:

A fashion brand uses augmented reality experiences in its app to allow users to virtually "try on" clothes before buying, enhancing the online shopping experience.

3. Influencer Marketing 2.0: Authentic and Long-Term Collaborations

Influencer marketing has evolved beyond simple sporadic collaborations. Brands are looking for long-term partnerships with influencers who authentically align with their values and messages. Authenticity and transparency have become key in these relationships, building trust between followers and the brand.

Practical Example:

A beauty product company collaborates with an influencer who has demonstrated a genuine commitment to the brand over time, sharing real experiences and results with the product.

4. Optimized User Experiences for Mobile Devices: Mobility at the Core

With the continued growth of mobile device usage, brands are focusing their efforts on optimizing the user experience for mobile platforms. From responsive websites to agile apps, the mobile approach is essential to reach an always-on audience.

Practical Example:

An e-commerce platform has developed an application that not only facilitates shopping, but also provides exclusive content and offers for users who interact primarily through mobile devices.

5. Marketing Automation: Efficiency and Personalization at Scale

Marketing automation is no longer simply about scheduling social media posts. It now involves creating complex workflows that personalize communication at every stage of the sales funnel. From personalized emails to automated responses based on user behavior, automation enables personalization at scale.

Practical Example:

A software company uses automation to send personalized emails based on user interactions on its website, delivering relevant content and exclusive offers.

The Inextricable Relationship Between Digital Marketing and Artificial Intelligence

Artificial intelligence (AI) has become the catalyst for many of these trends, empowering personalization, predictive analytics and automation capabilities. The intelligent integration of AI into digital marketing strategies is essential to keep up with the demands of an increasingly sophisticated audience.

1. Predictive Analytics for Strategic Anticipation

AI enables the analysis of large data sets to forecast consumer trends and behaviors. From anticipating product preferences to identifying optimal times for specific campaigns, predictive analytics drives informed strategic decisions.

2. AI-Powered Chatbots for Personalized Interactions

Chatbots have evolved beyond predefined responses. AI enables chatbots to understand natural language, adapting to user queries in a personalized way. This not only improves customer service efficiency, but also provides more meaningful interactions.

3. AI-Assisted Content Creation for Efficiency and Relevance

AI is being used to create content more efficiently and relevantly. From automatically generating ad copy to creating personalized images, AI assistance is optimizing content production, enabling rapid response to market demands.

The Labyrinth of Digital Marketing in the Age of Transformation

The intersection between digital marketing and artificial intelligence marks a new era of possibilities and challenges. The ability to adapt quickly to emerging trends and leverage AI tools will be critical to success in this ever-changing maze. As we plunge into this era of digital transformation, the synergy between innovative digital marketing strategies and artificial intelligence presents itself as the path to excellence and relevance in the contemporary digital landscape.

Differentiated Sales Impact: An Analysis by Continents and Ethnicities

The pandemic has not only transformed the way businesses operate, but has also left a differentiated impact on global sales trends. Analyzing variations by continent and considering the diversity of ethnic groups reveals intriguing patterns that shed light on how sales have evolved post-pandemic.

- **North America: Rapid E-Commerce Adoption and Focus on Virtual Experiences**

Booming e-commerce:

North America has experienced rapid adoption of e-commerce, with a significant increase in online transactions. The convenience and security associated with online shopping has led to a lasting shift in consumer preferences.

Virtual Experiences in Entertainment and Retail:

There has been an increase in demand for virtual experiences in sectors such as entertainment and retail. Companies have innovated by creating virtual events and showcases, providing consumers with a more immersive experience from the comfort of their homes.

- **Europe: Resurgence of Local and Sustainable Consumption**

Focus on Local Consumption:

Europe has witnessed a resurgence in the focus on local consumption. Consumers increasingly value the connection with local producers, which has led to an increase in shopping at local markets and the promotion of regional products.

Preference for Sustainable Practices:

Environmental awareness has led to increased preference for products and brands that adopt sustainable practices. Companies that communicate their commitment to sustainability have experienced growth in customer loyalty.

- **Asia: Technological Innovation and the Rise of Social Commerce**

Leadership in Technological Innovation:

Asia has led the way in technological innovation in sales. From augmented reality applications to contactless payment solutions, the region has been fertile ground for the adoption of emerging technologies that enhance the customer experience.

Social Commerce in Ascenso:

Social commerce has experienced a significant boom in Asia. Social networking platforms that integrate direct shopping capabilities have gained popularity, allowing users to discover and purchase products without leaving the application.

- **Latin America: Resilience in Digital Adoption and Focus on Personal Interactions**

Resilience in Digital Adoption:

Despite economic challenges, Latin America has shown resilience in digital adoption. Small businesses have turned to online platforms to reach new customers, highlighting the importance of digital presence even in adverse economic environments.

Focus on Personal Interactions:

While digital adoption has grown, sales are still largely driven by personal interactions and close relationships. Latino culture values personal connections in business transactions, and successful companies have found ways to balance digitization with a human touch.

- **Africa: Local Empowerment and Adaptation to the Digital Economy**

Local Empowerment through the Digital Economy:

Africa has experienced local empowerment through the digital economy. E-commerce platforms designed to cater to local markets have enabled small businesses to reach a wider audience and compete in a digital environment.

Innovation in Payment Methods:

Innovation in payment methods has been key to the adoption of the digital economy in Africa. Solutions such as mobile wallets and contactless payments have facilitated secure and efficient transactions.

Impact on Ethnic and Social Groups: Important Considerations

Digital Inclusion Challenges:

Globally, digital inclusion challenges persist, affecting certain ethnic and social groups. Ensuring equitable access to technology and digital skills remains an imperative to avoid widening existing gaps.

Potential for Offer Diversification:

Companies that recognize diversity in their audiences and tailor their offerings accordingly have the potential to capitalize on growth opportunities. Inclusive marketing strategies can create stronger connections with diverse ethnic and social groups.

Future Strategies

Differentiated analysis by continent and ethnic group reveals the complexity and diversity of post-pandemic sales trends. Future strategies will need to be flexible and adaptive, recognizing the importance of personalization, technological innovation and authentic audience connection. The ability of companies to understand and embrace diversity in their strategies will be crucial to thrive in this new global sales landscape.

The New Landscape: Adaptive Strategies for Businesses in the Post-Pandemic Era.

After examining the differentiated impact on sales by continent and ethnicity, it is clear that adaptability and an understanding of diverse market dynamics are essential to business success in the post-pandemic era. Here, I will present some key strategies that companies can consider to navigate the new global sales landscape:

1. Focus on Contextual Personalization:

Developing Personalized Experiences: Companies must move beyond demographic-based personalization and focus on providing contextually relevant experiences. Real-time adaptation to individual needs and preferences will strengthen the connection with the audience.

Integration of Emerging Technologies:

Adoption of Disruptive Technologies: The integration of emerging technologies such as augmented reality, artificial intelligence and virtual reality can be a key differentiator. These technologies not only enhance the customer experience, but also open up new opportunities for engagement.

3. Strengthening of Electronic Commerce Strategies:

Online Platform Optimization: Companies must continue to strengthen their e-commerce strategies, improving ease of navigation, security and transaction efficiency. Investing in secure payment solutions and implementing augmented reality features can further boost online sales.

4. Sustainability and Environmental Awareness:

Commitment to Sustainable Practices: A focus on sustainable practices not only responds to growing environmental awareness, but can also appeal to a wider audience. Effectively communicating sustainability efforts can become a deciding factor for consumers.

5. Strategies for Inclusion and Authentic Connection:

Inclusive and Authentic Campaigns: Inclusion and authenticity in marketing strategies are critical. Companies should celebrate diversity in their campaigns and seek authentic connections with consumers, recognizing the richness of cultural and social experiences.

6. Equitable Digitalization:

Digital Access and Education: To address digital inclusion gaps, companies can contribute by providing equitable access to technology and promoting digital education programs. This not only broadens the consumer base, but also contributes to equity in the digital age.

7. Continuous Analysis and Adaptation:

Trend Monitoring and Consumer Data: The ability to continuously adapt is based on the constant monitoring of market trends and the collection of consumer data. The implementation of predictive analytics and artificial intelligence tools will facilitate data-driven decision making.

Challenges and Opportunities: Embracing the Future with Resilience

As companies embark on implementing these strategies, they must also be prepared to face challenges. Business resilience in the post-pandemic era involves recognizing that the path to success can be dynamic and will require continuous adjustments.

Potential Challenges:

> Ethical Challenges in the Use of Emerging Technologies.
> Intense Competition in the Digital Space.
> Adaptation to Regulations and Changes in the Commercial Environment.
> Emerging Opportunities
> Creation of New Business Models.
> Global Strategic Partnerships.

Innovation in Customer Experiences.

In conclusion, companies that embrace flexibility, innovation and authentic connection with their audiences will be better positioned to thrive in this new global retail landscape. Business resilience will be an invaluable tool in the journey into the future, where the ability to continually adapt will be key to staying relevant and successful.

The New Era of Opportunities and Challenges

This comprehensive analysis of the differentiated impact on sales by continent and ethnicity reveals a complex and dynamic landscape that defines the post-pandemic era. The adaptive strategies presented address emerging trends and offer an approach for companies to not only survive, but thrive in this new environment.

Clear Opportunities:

✓ Contextual personalization and the integration of emerging technologies offer opportunities to create deeper connections with the audience.
✓ Business resilience can translate into competitive advantage, especially when embracing sustainability and inclusion.
✓ Intricate Challenges:
✓ Intense competition and ethical challenges in the use of emerging technologies require a careful balance.
✓ Adapting to changing regulations and managing digital transformation present ongoing challenges.

Future Projection: The Transformation Continues

Looking ahead, we envision an era where companies will be shaped by their ability to adapt, innovate and be authentic. The convergence of digital marketing, artificial intelligence and changing sales dynamics will give way to:

- Customer Experience Focused Companies:
- Customer experience will be at the core of business strategy. Companies that understand and anticipate their customers' needs through contextual personalization will lead the way.
- Positive Impact and Sustainability:
- Companies that adopt sustainable practices and communicate their commitment to corporate social responsibility will attract a more aware and engaged customer base.
- Global Collaboration and New Business Models:
- Strategic collaboration at the global level will intensify, and companies will explore innovative business models to address shared challenges and seize global opportunities.

Together Towards Excellence

At the intersection of digital marketing, artificial intelligence and changing sales trends, there is an invitation for companies to not only survive but thrive in this new era. Adaptability and resilience become currency, and authentic connection with the audience is the bond that will ensure success.

The evolution of sales is not only a reflection of changing consumer behavior, but also an opportunity to redefine the relationship between companies and their customers. In this journey, ethics and responsibility become guiding lights, ensuring that the transformation is inclusive and benefits everyone.

The post-pandemic era has not only challenged us, but also provided us with a blank sheet of paper full of limitless possibilities. At the intersection of technology and humanity, companies have the opportunity to forge a path to excellence, where innovation, inclusion and authenticity are the driving forces.

Continuous transformation will be the constant, and those who embrace change with courage and vision will be best positioned to lead the future of digital sales and marketing. In this exciting journey into the unknown, the key will be to not only navigate the waves of change, but also to be bold architects of a future where excellence is the norm and the possibilities are truly limitless.

Which countries in the world are emerging to lead the new era of trade?

Based on the trends observed in recent years and projecting the impact of changes in marketing and sales, we can identify some countries by region that are positioned to lead in the new commercial era according to their technological advances and adaptation policies.

North America: United States and Canada Consolidate Digital Dominance

United States: With a strong technology infrastructure, a diverse consumer market and the presence of technology giants, the United States will continue to lead in the adoption of emerging technologies and digital marketing strategies.

Canada: Like its southern neighbor, Canada will benefit from its advanced digital connectivity and economic diversification. The adaptability of Canadian companies will be key to capitalizing on emerging opportunities.

Europe: Germany and Scandinavia at the Forefront of Sustainability

Germany: With a robust manufacturing industry and a focus on sustainability, Germany will excel in implementing responsible business practices and adopting innovative technologies.

Scandinavian countries (Sweden, Norway, Denmark, Finland): These nations, known for their quality of life and environmental awareness, will lead in integrating sustainable practices into business strategies and creating personalized experiences for consumers.

Asia: China and Singapore Boost Technology Innovation

China: With its rapid technological development, China will continue to lead innovation in digital sales, artificial intelligence and e-commerce. Chinese companies will look to expand globally and diversify their offerings.

Singapore: As Asia's financial and technological center, Singapore will be a key player in the adoption of emerging technologies. Its strategic position will make it a hub for global business collaboration.

Latin America: Brazil and Mexico Navigate Digital Adoption with Resilience

Brazil: Despite economic challenges, Brazil will show resilience in digital adoption. Its rich culture and demographic diversity will provide opportunities for inclusive and authentic marketing strategies.

Mexico: With a growing young population and a growing middle class, Mexico will excel in adopting new technologies and connecting authentically with consumers.

Africa: Nigeria and South Africa Lead the Way in Digital Momentum

Nigeria: With a young population and increasing Internet penetration, Nigeria will be a leader in the adoption of digital technologies and the creation of innovative business models.

South Africa: As the continent's most advanced economy, South Africa will capitalize on digitalization to strengthen key sectors such as e-commerce and tourism.

South America: New Players Emerge in the Trade Revolution

In addition to Brazil and Mexico, which stand out for their resilience and digital adoption, there are three more countries in South America that are projected to be significant players in the post-pandemic business revolution:

Argentina: Innovation and Diversification in Emerging Markets

Technological Innovation: Argentina, with its vibrant technological scene, would position itself as a center of innovation, especially in the development of technological applications and solutions to optimize marketing and sales strategies.

Diversification into Emerging Industries: Diversification into emerging sectors, such as fintech and renewable energy, would provide opportunities for business growth, and digital marketing strategies will be key to positioning these industries globally.

Colombia: Boosting e-Commerce and Global Connection

E-Commerce Growth: Colombia will experience significant growth in e-commerce, taking advantage of its increasing Internet penetration and young population. Digital marketing strategies focused on customer experience will be crucial to take advantage of this boom.

Global Connection in Latin America: Given its strategic location, Colombia will consolidate its position as a global connection hub in Latin America, facilitating international trade and business collaborations.

Chile: Leadership in Sustainability and Customer Experience

Commitment to Sustainability: Chile, with its focus on renewable energy and sustainability, will lead the way in incorporating responsible business practices. Marketing strategies that communicate this commitment will resonate strongly with conscious consumers.

Differentiated Customer Experience: Chilean companies will stand out by focusing on customer experience, using emerging technologies to offer personalized and authentic interactions.

Peru: Sustainable Takeoff in the New Commercial Era

E-Commerce Development: Sustained growth: Peru will experience sustained growth in e-commerce, driven by increased connectivity and growing digital acceptance among consumers.

with its rich cultural heritage and forward-thinking approach, is poised to merge tradition and modernity in the new era of commerce. Marketing strategies that celebrate authenticity, sustainability and forward momentum will be critical to the success of Peruvian companies in this exciting global business chapter. At the intersection of its deep-rooted traditions and forward-looking vision, Peru becomes a key player on the South American and global trade stage.

South America: A Continent Diverse in Opportunities

South America, with its cultural and economic diversity, presents a number of opportunities in the new commercial era. Each country has its unique set of strengths, and the key to success will lie in business resilience, constant innovation and authentic connection with local and international consumers. Together, these six countries-Brazil, Mexico, Argentina, Colombia, Chile and Peru-reflect the region's richness and promise in the changing global trade landscape.

A Global Overview: Shaping the Future of Trade Across Regions

So far, we have explored the post-pandemic business dynamics in South America, but the global scenario is also shaping up with significant changes. By analyzing different regions of the world, it is possible to draw a complete picture of how marketing and sales strategies will evolve in the new era. Let's take a look at how each region is shaping up:

1. North America: Innovation and Continued Digital Dominance

United States and Canada: Technological innovation will continue to be a key pillar. Marketing strategies in personalization, artificial intelligence and engaging digital experiences will consolidate the position of these nations as undisputed leaders in the digital space.

2. Europe: Sustainability and Adaptation to Climate Change

Germany and Scandinavia: Sustainability will be key. Marketing strategies focused on environmental and social responsibility will resonate strongly. Adaptation to climate change will drive emerging industries and new business models.

3. Asia: Technological Innovation and Sustainable Globalization

China and Singapore: Technological innovation will continue to be the hallmark. Marketing strategies in artificial intelligence, e-commerce and global connectivity will consolidate these nations as technological and commercial hubs.

4. Africa: Digitalization and Entrepreneurship

Nigeria and South Africa: Digitalization will be a key driver. Marketing strategies that encourage digital entrepreneurship and financial inclusion will be key to economic development. A boom in the adoption of emerging technologies is expected.

5. Middle East: Economic Diversification and Sustainable Tourism

United Arab Emirates and Qatar: Economic diversification will be a strategic focus. Marketing strategies that highlight the diversity of sectors, from sustainable tourism to technology, will lead the way to a more robust economic future.

6. Oceania: Connectivity and Environmental Conservation

Australia and New Zealand: Digital connectivity will remain key. Marketing strategies focused on digital experiences and environmental conservation will resonate with an aware and engaged population.

7. Antarctica: Conservation and Sustainable Science

Antarctic Research Stations: Environmental conservation and sustainable science will be the cornerstones. Marketing strategies that communicate conservation efforts and the value of scientific research will gain relevance.

Towards a Global Future of Opportunity and Collaboration

In the global fabric of commerce, each region brings its uniqueness and perspective. The convergence of marketing strategies focused on sustainability, technology and emotional connection with the audience will mark a new chapter in the retail world.

Global collaboration will be essential, and companies that can adapt to the specific needs of each region while maintaining a global vision will be best positioned to thrive in this exciting future. Let this diverse landscape be the catalyst for a business era that celebrates innovation, sustainability and global connection!

Adaptability Defines Commercial Success

In the new era of commerce, adaptability and an understanding of changing market dynamics are essential for success. While these countries have particular advantages, true differentiation will come from the ability of companies to embrace innovation, sustainability and authenticity in their business strategies. Global collaboration and an understanding of local needs will be critical factors for sustainable leadership in this exciting new commercial chapter.

CHAPTER III

Social Networking: The Future of Digital Marketing and the Challenges of Employment in the Digital Age

The digital age has radically transformed the world of marketing. Companies can now reach their customers in ways never before possible, thanks to advances in digital technology.

However, this transformation has also brought with it new challenges for marketers. In an increasingly digital world, it is essential for marketers to stay on top of the latest trends and technologies. They must also be able to think creatively and strategically to develop marketing campaigns that are effective in the digital world.

Digital marketing trends

In the future, digital marketing will continue to evolve as new technologies and trends emerge. Some of the most important trends that are expected to dominate digital marketing in the coming years include:

Personalization: Personalization will be key to digital marketing success in the future. Companies will be able to use data and analytics to create personalized marketing experiences for each customer.

Automation: Marketing automation will also be a major trend. Companies will be able to use automated tools for tasks such as content creation, social media management and data analysis.

Innovation: Innovation will be critical to digital marketing success. Companies that stay on the cutting edge of the latest trends and technologies will be the most successful.

Employment challenges in the digital era

The digital transformation has also had an impact on the labor market. As companies adopt new technologies, some tasks traditionally performed by humans are being automated.

This has led to job losses in some sectors, such as production and customer service. However, it has also created new jobs in other sectors, such as technology and digital marketing.

Companies that want to succeed in the digital age must focus on developing the skills and talent they need to thrive in this new environment. This includes digital skills, critical thinking skills and problem-solving skills.

The Future of Digital Marketing

The future of digital marketing is bright. Companies that adapt to the latest trends and technologies will be the most successful so it is important to take the following aspects:

- **The Fundamental Role of Social Networks:**

Social networks have become central pillars of digital marketing, serving as platforms where brands can build authentic connections with their audiences. From targeted advertising to user engagement, social networks have evolved beyond simple promotional channels to become dynamic spaces for interaction.

- **Optimistic Perspective on Employment in the Digital Age:**

Despite initial fears about automation and artificial intelligence, the digital revolution has also created new employment opportunities. Roles in digital marketing, social media management and data analytics are booming. Human creativity remains essential for creating meaningful content and emotionally connecting with audiences.

- **Challenges:**

However, we cannot ignore the challenges that the digital age presents to employment. Automation of routine tasks can lead to the obsolescence of some jobs, and the speed of change can be overwhelming for those who do not keep up to date. It is crucial to address the skills gap and ensure that education and training evolve at the same pace as technology.

- **The Importance of Continuous Learning:**

In this context, the need for a constant commitment to continuous learning is emphasized. Professionals must be willing to acquire new skills and adapt to technological innovations. Educational institutions and companies have a crucial role to play in facilitating this process by providing training and development opportunities.

- **Ethics in Digital Marketing:**

As digital marketing expands, there is a critical need to address ethical issues. From consumer privacy to transparency in the use of data, brands must operate with integrity to build and maintain public trust.

The Evolution of Digital Marketing:

In the last decade, we have witnessed an amazing transformation in the world of digital marketing. Social networks are no longer mere digital storefronts and have become interactive forums where authenticity and engagement are commonplace. Brands are no longer just looking to sell products, but to build long-term relationships with their customers through relevant content and meaningful experiences.

- **The Rise of Artificial Intelligence**:

Artificial intelligence (AI) has been a key catalyst in this revolution. From recommendation algorithms to advanced data analytics, AI powers digital marketing strategies, enabling unprecedented personalization. Brands can anticipate consumer needs and deliver more relevant and persuasive messages.

- **Employment in the Digital Age:**

Despite initial fears about job losses due to automation, the reality is more complex. The digital age has created new job opportunities in roles that did not even exist a decade ago. Social media specialists, data analysts, and artificial intelligence experts are now critical pieces in the labor ecosystem.

- **Challenges to be faced:**

However, the speed of change also presents significant challenges. Automation can make certain jobs redundant, and adapting to new technologies can be daunting for some. The skills gap is a reality, and it is crucial to address it proactively through education and training programs.

- **The Role of the Content and Community Manager**:

Within this scenario, the role of the content and community manager becomes even more crucial. These professionals are the architects of the brand narrative, building bridges between companies and their audiences. Human creativity and the ability to understand emotions remain irreplaceable in the digital era.

- **Ethics and Transparency:**

As we harness the power of artificial intelligence and social media, ethics in digital marketing becomes a central issue. Consumer privacy, transparency in the use of data and honesty in marketing practices are essential to building and maintaining public trust.

- **Commitment to Continuous Learning:**

The key to success in the digital age is a constant commitment to continuous learning. Both professionals and companies must be willing to evolve and acquire new skills. Educational institutions and organizations have a responsibility to provide resources and opportunities for this continuous development.

- **Looking to the Future:**

As we move into a digital future, the intersection of marketing, artificial intelligence and social media will continue to define our employment landscape. Maintaining a balance between technological innovation, ethics and personal development will be crucial to making the most of the opportunities and overcoming the challenges ahead.

Ultimately, digital marketing, driven by artificial intelligence and framed by social media, promises an exciting future full of possibilities. With an ethical approach and a commitment to continuous learning, we can build a digital environment that benefits businesses, professionals and consumers alike.

Employment Challenges in the Digital Age:

Despite the burgeoning opportunities in digital marketing, we cannot overlook the intrinsic challenges that the digital age poses to employment. Automation, driven by artificial intelligence, has raised concerns about the loss of traditional jobs. Roles that previously required routine skills may find themselves at risk, underscoring the urgency of constant adaptation.

- **The Skills Gap in the Digital Revolution:**

The rapid evolution of technology has resulted in a skills gap that affects professionals and businesses alike. The ability to keep up with the latest trends and technologies has become a key competency in the competitive world of digital marketing.

- **Education and Continuing Education:**

To address these challenges, it is imperative that educational institutions and companies offer continuing education programs. Professionals must be encouraged to acquire new skills, and organizations must facilitate environments that foster innovation and continuous learning.

- **The Ethical Impact of Digital Marketing:**

In addition to job challenges, digital marketing also faces significant ethical questions. Massive data collection and precise audience segmentation raise concerns about consumer privacy. It is imperative that brands operate with transparency and respect ethical boundaries to maintain public trust.

- **Key Roles in the Future of Digital Marketing:**

In this challenging landscape, certain roles emerge as cornerstones for the future of digital marketing. Content and community managers, with their ability to build authentic relationships and engaging narratives, become essential. These professionals humanize brands in an increasingly digitized world.

- **The Importance of Human Creativity:**

Although artificial intelligence plays a crucial role in automating tasks and personalizing content, human creativity remains irreplaceable. Innovative ideas, empathy and understanding of emotions are elements that no algorithm can fully replicate.

- **Preparing for the Future:**

In conclusion, as we explore the future of digital marketing in the age of social media and artificial intelligence, it is critical to take a proactive approach. The opportunities for growth are vast, but only those willing to embrace change and engage in continuous learning can take full advantage of this constantly evolving landscape.

As we face challenges and seize opportunities, it is essential to remember that the human factor remains the driving force behind every successful marketing strategy. By merging technology with creativity and ethics, we are building a future where digital marketing not only thrives, but also becomes a positive force for society as a whole.

The Fusion of Technology and Creativity:

In this new paradigm of digital marketing, the harmonious fusion of technology and creativity emerges as the key to success. Artificial intelligence-driven tools and social media platforms provide an infinite canvas for creative expression. Brands that understand how to leverage these tools ethically and authentically will be leaders in this exciting journey.

- **The Strategic Role of the Content and Community Manager:**

At the forefront of this convergence is the content and community manager. Their strategic role goes beyond publishing content; it is about building genuine communities, understanding the subtleties of human interaction and creating narratives that resonate with the audience. In this digital future, these professionals are the architects of deep and meaningful connections.

- **Ethical Challenges and Responsibilities:**

As we move forward, it is imperative to address ethical challenges with resolve. Massive data collection and extreme personalization require clear boundaries and a privacy-centric approach. Brands have a responsibility to be transparent in their practices, and marketers must lead with integrity in every step they take.

- **Education as a Pillar of Change:**

At the heart of this revolution, education emerges as a fundamental pillar. Continuing education is not only a means to stay current, but a vehicle for personal and professional transformation. Educational institutions and companies must collaborate to create programs that foster adaptability and the acquisition of relevant skills.

- **The Future of Employment:**

Despite the challenges, the future of employment in the digital age holds exciting opportunities. New, previously unimaginable roles are emerging, and creative and agile minds are increasingly in demand. The ability to understand consumer psychology, tell compelling stories and navigate the digital world will be essential.

Ultimately, this ever-changing landscape not only redefines digital marketing, but also transforms the way we live and work. Creativity, ethics and continuous learning rise as the pillars that will guide professionals and brands to success in this new era.

The Adaptability Challenge

At the heart of this digital revolution lies the fundamental challenge of adaptability. Marketers and sales professionals, who have embraced technology and artificial intelligence, are the architects of a new paradigm. The ability to adapt to the constant evolution of digital platforms and marketing strategies defines the difference between relevance and obsolescence.

- **Technological Innovation and Personal Development:**

As new technologies emerge at a dizzying pace, it is crucial to recognize that technological innovation and personal development go hand in hand. Continuing education should not only focus on the acquisition of technical skills, but also on the cultivation of soft skills such as creativity, empathy and emotional intelligence.

- **Strategies for Addressing the Skills Gap:**

Addressing the skills gap requires synergistic collaboration between governments, businesses and educators. Adaptive training programs, online courses, and industry collaborations are essential to equip the workforce with the necessary skills. Companies, in turn, must adopt a proactive mindset to foster a continuous learning environment.

The Ethical Transformation of Digital Marketing:

The digital marketing of the future will not only be defined by advanced technology, but also by an ethical transformation. The responsibility of brands to safeguard consumer privacy and operate with transparency will be central. Marketers must become champions of digital ethics, guiding their organizations toward practices that prioritize integrity and customer trust.

- **Human-Machine Collaboration in the Marketing of the Future:**

As we move forward, human-machine collaboration will become a cornerstone of future marketing. Artificial intelligence may boost efficiency in task automation, but human creativity and intuition will remain irreplaceable in strategic decision making and emotional connection with the audience.

- **The Pivotal Role of Content and Community Managers:**

The roles of content and community managers will establish themselves as crucial pivots in this digital age. Their ability to tell authentic stories, encourage engagement and build strong communities will be essential for brands looking to establish a meaningful presence in an increasingly connected world.

- **The Future, a Blank Canvas:**

The future of marketing and sales looks like a blank canvas full of possibilities. While we face significant challenges, we are also immersed in a period of unprecedented innovation. With the right combination of adaptability, ethics and human-machine collaboration, we can paint a vibrant and sustainable portrait for digital marketing in the age of artificial intelligence and social media.

In this ongoing journey into the unknown, let's remember that, as marketers, we are storytellers, community builders and, above all, agents of change at the intersection of the human and the digital.

In concrete terms, the future of digital marketing could look like this:

Marketing campaigns will become more personalized and relevant to customers. Companies will use data and analytics to understand their customers' needs and preferences, and create marketing experiences that are relevant to each individual customer.

Marketing automation will become more pervasive. Companies will use automated tools for tasks such as content creation, social media management and data analysis. This will free marketers to focus on more strategic tasks.

Marketing will become more omnichannel. Companies will use a variety of channels to reach their customers, including social media, email, search engines and display advertising.

Marketing will become more data-driven. Companies will use data to understand customer behavior and optimize their marketing campaigns.

These are just some of the changes that are coming in the future of digital marketing. Companies that adapt to these trends will be the most successful in the digital age.

CHAPTER IV
How artificial intelligence influences modern

<u>marketing</u>

Artificial intelligence (AI) is the ability of machines to mimic some human cognitive functions, such as perception, reasoning, learning and problem solving. AI has become an invaluable tool for marketers, enabling them to better understand their audiences, deliver what they need and what they are interested in, and optimize their strategies and campaigns.

AI can be applied in different areas of marketing, such as predictive analytics, content generation, customer relations and digital advertising. Let's take a look at some examples:

Predictive analytics: AI can process and analyze large volumes of data at a speed and scale that would be impossible for a human. This allows it to identify consumer patterns, trends and behaviors, and predict their actions or inactions. Thus, marketers can anticipate the needs and preferences of their audience, and offer personalized and relevant products or services.

Content generation: AI can create content automatically, using natural language processing (NLP) and deep learning algorithms. This content can range from simple texts, such as headlines, descriptions or summaries, to more complex texts, such as articles, reports or books. AI can also generate other types of content, such as images, videos or audios. This content can be used to attract, inform or entertain users, and to improve brands' SEO.

Customer relationships: AI can interact with customers in natural language, using tools such as chatbots, virtual assistants or voice platforms. These tools can provide fast, efficient and personalized customer service, 24/7. They can also collect valuable information about customers, such as their personal data, opinions, questions or complaints, and use it to improve user experience and loyalty.

Digital advertising: AI can optimize digital advertising campaigns, using machine learning and reinforcement learning algorithms. These algorithms can select the best channels, formats, messages and times to display ads, and adjust them in real time based on performance and user feedback. Thus, marketers can maximize the return on investment (ROI) and reach of their campaigns.

How is AI influencing modern marketing?

AIs are having a significant impact on marketing in a number of ways, including:

Personalization: AI enables companies to personalize their marketing messages to reach customers more effectively. For example, AI can be used to identify customers' interests based on their behavioral data, such as their purchase history or social media interactions. This allows companies to create content and offers that are more relevant to each individual customer.

Automation: AI can automate many marketing tasks that were previously performed by humans, such as data collection, data analysis and reporting. This frees marketers to focus on more strategic and creative tasks.

Prediction: AI can be used to predict customer behavior, allowing companies to optimize their marketing strategies. For example, AI can be used to predict which products or services customers are likely to buy in the future. This allows companies to adapt their offerings to customers' changing needs.

The future of marketers in the age of AI

AI does not come to replace marketers, but to complement and empower them as they can perform repetitive, routine or tedious tasks, and free up time and resources for marketers to focus on more creative, strategic or emotional tasks.

However, AI also poses new challenges and changes for marketers, who must adapt to new technologies and new consumer demands. Some of these challenges and changes are:

Continuing education: Marketers must keep abreast of the latest developments and trends in the field of AI, and learn how to use the tools and methods it offers. They must also develop new skills and competencies, such as critical thinking, data analysis, project management and effective communication.

Multidisciplinary collaboration: Marketing professionals must work in teams with other professionals from different areas, such as computer science, engineering, design or psychology. These teams must be able to integrate human vision and machine vision, and take advantage of the synergies between the two.

Ethics and responsibility: Marketers should be aware of the risks and ethical implications of using AI, and act responsibly and transparently. Some of these risks include data privacy and security, bias and discrimination, manipulation and misinformation, or loss of control and trust.

New marketing trends with AI in the coming years

AI is constantly evolving and offers new possibilities and opportunities for marketing. Some of the trends that are shaping up for the future are:

Conversational marketing: Conversational marketing is based on dialogue between brands and customers, using tools such as chatbots, virtual assistants or voice platforms. These tools make it possible to offer a more human, personalized and close customer service, and to generate a relationship of trust and loyalty.

Emotional marketing: Emotional marketing focuses on the emotions and feelings of customers, using tools such as facial recognition, voice analysis and neuromarketing. These tools make it possible to measure and analyze customers' reactions and emotional responses to brand stimuli, and to adapt messages and offers to their moods and motivations.

Hyper-personalized marketing: Hyper-personalized marketing is marketing that adapts as much as possible to the characteristics, preferences and behaviors of each customer, using tools such as machine learning, big data and advanced segmentation. These tools make it possible to create detailed and dynamic customer profiles and offer them unique and memorable experiences.

What skills does a marketer need in the age of AI?

Artificial intelligence (AI) is a technology that is transforming marketing and requires marketers to constantly adapt and update. Some of the skills needed by marketers in the AI era are:

Technical skills: Marketers must know and handle the tools and methods offered by AI, such as data analysis, content generation, customer relationship or digital advertising. They must also know how to design and optimize prompts, which are the requests made to AI to obtain the desired results.

Analytical skills: Marketers must be able to interpret and leverage the data provided by AI, and to extract insights and conclusions that help them make strategic decisions and improve the performance of their campaigns.

Creative skills: Marketers must be creative and innovative, and use AI as a source of inspiration and support, but not as a substitute for their own vision and judgment. They must also know how to generate engaging, personalized and relevant content for their audience, using AI as a complementary tool.

Communication skills: Marketers must know how to communicate with AI, using clear, precise and natural language, and how to communicate with customers, using AI as a channel or an intermediary. They must also know how to convey the value and benefits of AI to their stakeholders, and how to build trust and credibility in its use.

Collaborative skills: Marketers must work in teams with other professionals from different areas, such as computer science, engineering, design or psychology, and know how to integrate human and machine vision. They must also be open to learning and feedback, and willing to share their knowledge and experience with AI.

Ethical skills: Marketers must be aware of the risks and ethical implications of using AI, and act responsibly and transparently. They must also respect privacy and data security, avoid bias and discrimination, and prevent manipulation and misinformation.

These are some of the skills that marketers need in the age of AI, but they are not the only ones. This is because it is a constantly evolving technology and offers new possibilities and opportunities for marketing. Therefore, professionals must keep abreast of the latest developments and trends, and be prepared to adapt and learn continuously.

What are the ethical risks of artificial intelligence in marketing?

Artificial intelligence (AI) is a technology that offers great benefits for marketing, but it also poses significant ethical challenges. Some of these challenges are:

Privacy and data security: AI relies on the collection and analysis of customer data, which can violate their privacy and expose them to risks of theft or misuse of their information. Companies must obtain customer consent, comply with legal regulations, and protect data with appropriate security measures.

Algorithmic bias and discrimination: AI can reproduce or amplify hidden biases in data or algorithms, which can affect marketing personalization and segmentation, and lead to discrimination or exclusion of certain customer groups. Companies should avoid or correct these biases, and promote fairness and diversity in marketing.

Manipulation and transparency of customer behavior: AI can influence customer behavior, using techniques such as neuromarketing, emotional marketing or conversational marketing, which can affect their autonomy and choice. Companies must be transparent and honest about the use of AI, and respect the rights and interests of customers.

How can biases in AI be avoided?

Biases in AI are distortions or unfairness that can affect data, algorithms, or AI outcomes, and can have negative consequences for human rights, equity, or inclusion. Some strategies to avoid or mitigate biases in AI include:

Ensure diversity in data sets: Data is the raw material of AI, and the quality and reliability of models and predictions depend on it. Therefore, it is important that the data is representative of reality and of the diversity of the people and contexts to which it is applied. It is also important that the data are clean, up-to-date and correctly labeled.

Perform rigorous testing and evaluation: Before implementing or deploying an AI system, it is necessary to perform tests and evaluations to identify and correct possible biases or errors. These tests should include different scenarios, use cases and user groups, and measure the impact and performance of the AI system. Periodic monitoring and review of the AI system is also necessary to detect and fix emerging problems or changes in the environment.

Provide human oversight: AI should not replace human judgment or responsibility, but complement and enhance it. Therefore, there needs to be human oversight that monitors and validates AI processes and outcomes, and can intervene or correct if necessary. This oversight must be performed by competent, ethical and diverse individuals who can bring different perspectives and values to the table.

Ensure transparency and explainability of AI systems: Transparency and explainability are key to generate trust and credibility in AI, and to facilitate accountability and user participation. Therefore, AI systems need to be transparent about how they work, their objectives, their data sources, their decision criteria and their possible limitations or risks. It is also necessary for AI systems to

IA are explainable, i.e., they can provide reasons or justifications for their actions or recommendations, and can respond to users' questions or doubts.

Collect and analyze brain data: AI can process and analyze large volumes of brain data obtained through techniques such as functional magnetic resonance imaging (fMRI) or electroencephalography (EEG). This data can measure consumers' emotions, attention and memory to marketing stimuli, and generate valuable insights for the design of more effective campaigns.

Personalize the consumer experience: AI can tailor marketing content and promotions based on consumer-specific data, such as preferences, behaviors and moods. Thus, a more relevant and personalized experience can be offered, generating a greater emotional connection and loyalty.

Predicting consumer behavior: AI can use brain data and other relevant data to predict consumer actions or inactions, such as purchase intent, satisfaction or abandonment. Thus, you can anticipate consumers' needs and wants, and offer them products or services that match their expectations

Philip Kotler is one of the most recognized experts in the field of marketing, and has written several books and articles on the influence of AI on marketing and the future consequences. some of the things Kotler says about AI and marketing are:

1. AI can help marketing teams become more efficient and effective by automating repetitive tasks and freeing up time for more creative and strategic tasks.
2. AI can enable greater analysis and prediction of data, identifying consumer patterns, trends and behaviors, and anticipating their needs and preferences.
3. AI can generate content automatically or assisted, creating texts, images, videos or audios that attract, inform or entertain users.
4. AI may displace workers in certain industries and increase the gap between the rich and the poor.
5. AI can lead to discrimination and a lack of transparency in decision making

Ray Kurzweil is one of the pioneers and visionaries of artificial intelligence (AI), a technology that enables machines to learn and perform tasks that require human intelligence. Kurzweil has written several books and articles on the future of humanity and technology, and has made numerous predictions, especially regarding nanotechnology and AI.

According to Kurzweil, AI will have a major impact on marketing, offering new possibilities and opportunities to better understand customers, personalize messages, optimize campaigns and improve results. Some of Kurzweil's predictions about AI and marketing are:

- ✓ AI will be truly intelligent and pass the Turing Test by 2029, and will merge with the human brain to power our abilities by 2045.
- ✓ AI can help marketing teams become more efficient and effective by automating repetitive tasks and freeing up time for more creative and strategic tasks.

- ✓ AI can enable greater analysis and prediction of data, identifying consumer patterns, trends and behaviors, and anticipating their needs and preferences.
- ✓ AI can generate content automatically or assisted, creating text, images, videos or audios that engage, inform or entertain users.
- ✓ AI can interact with customers in natural language, using tools such as chatbots, virtual assistants or voice platforms, and deliver fast, efficient and personalized customer service.
- ✓ AI can optimize digital advertising campaigns, selecting the best channels, formats, messages and times to display ads, and adjusting them in real time based on performance and user feedback.

However, AI also poses new challenges and risks for marketing, such as the displacement of workers, discrimination and lack of transparency in decision making, or loss of control and trust.

Kurzweil therefore advocates ethical and responsible AI that respects privacy and data security, avoids bias and discrimination, and is transparent and honest with customers.

Seth Godin: is one of the most influential referents in the marketing field, and has written several books and articles on how to create and spread ideas that make a difference.

According to Godin, marketing is about generating authentic connections with our audience, building lasting relationships and, most importantly, making people feel like they are part of something.

In the age of artificial intelligence (AI), a technology that enables machines to learn and perform tasks that require human intelligence, marketing faces new challenges and opportunities. AI can help marketing teams become more efficient and effective by automating repetitive tasks and freeing up time for more creative and strategic tasks.

AI can also enable greater analysis and prediction of data, identifying consumer patterns, trends and behaviors, and anticipating their needs and preferences. In addition, AI can generate content automatically or assisted, creating text, images, videos or audios that engage, inform or entertain users.

However, AI also poses new risks and ethical dilemmas, such as data privacy and security, algorithmic bias and discrimination, manipulation and transparency of customer behavior, or loss of control and trust.

For this reason, Godin advocates marketing based on permission and emotional connection, which respects the rights and interests of customers, and which offers them relevant and valuable content. For Godin, marketing is not about interrupting or persuading people, but about creating tribes around a brand or product, where followers become enthusiastic ambassadors who spread the message organically.

AI is a disruptive technology that is transforming modern marketing, offering great advantages and benefits for brands and customers. However, it also implies new challenges and changes for marketers, who must be prepared and updated to take advantage of its full potential. AI is not a threat, but an opportunity to create smarter, more creative and more human marketing.

CHAPTER V

The impact of artificial intelligence in the world: opportunities and challenges.

Artificial intelligence (AI) is one of the most disruptive and promising technologies of the 21st century. According to the PwC report1, AI could contribute $15.7 trillion to global GDP by 2030, an increase of 14%. However, AI also poses significant ethical, social, economic and labor challenges that require appropriate reflection and regulation. In this article, we will analyze the impact of AI on the world from different perspectives, as well as the opinions of experts speaking for and against this technology.

What is artificial intelligence and how has it evolved?

Artificial intelligence is defined as the ability of machines to perform tasks that normally require human intelligence, such as learning, reasoning, perception and decision making. AI is based on algorithms that are trained with data to recognize patterns and generate responses. There are different types of AI according to their degree of complexity and autonomy, from weak or specific AI, which is limited to a specific task, to strong or general AI, which aims to match or surpass human intelligence in all areas.

AI is not a recent phenomenon, but has its origins in the 1950s, when the term was coined and the first computer programs capable of playing chess or solving logic problems were developed. However, AI has experienced a breakthrough in recent years thanks to the development of computing, connectivity, storage and data analysis, which have enabled the creation of more powerful, versatile and accessible AI systems. Examples of current AI applications include virtual assistants, autonomous vehicles, facial recognition systems, chatbots, automatic translators and recommendation algorithms.

What benefits and opportunities does artificial intelligence offer?

AI offers multiple benefits and opportunities to improve quality of life, well-being, health, education, security, environment, innovation, competitiveness and economic growth. Some of the benefits and opportunities of AI are as follows:

- ✓ AI can increase productivity and process efficiency, reducing costs, errors and execution time. For example, AI can optimize supply chain management, logistics, transportation, agriculture, energy or manufacturing.
- ✓ AI can improve the quality and personalization of products and services, adapting them to customers' preferences, needs and expectations. For example, AI can deliver personalized, real-time content, offers, advice or customer service.
- ✓ AI can facilitate access to and democratization of information, knowledge, culture and education, eliminating geographical, linguistic, economic or social barriers. For example, AI can provide online learning platforms, massive open courses, automatic translation or access to digital content.
- ✓ AI can contribute to the prevention, diagnosis, treatment and monitoring of diseases, improving people's health and life expectancy. For example, AI can analyze medical images, detect anomalies, suggest treatments, monitor vital signs or facilitate telemedicine.
- ✓ AI can help solve global problems, such as climate change, poverty, hunger, inequality or conflict, by generating data, predicting scenarios, proposing solutions or mobilizing resources. For example, AI can monitor the state of the environment, predict natural disasters, optimize the use of resources, identify vulnerabilities or facilitate cooperation.

What risks and challenges does artificial intelligence pose?

- AI also poses risks and challenges that may affect human rights, ethics, security, privacy, justice, employment, education, culture, politics or the economy. Some of the risks and challenges of AI are as follows:
- AI can generate bias, discrimination, exclusion or unfairness, if the algorithms or the data that feed them reflect existing prejudices, stereotypes or inequalities in society. For example, AI can discriminate against people based on their gender, race, age, sexual orientation, religion or disability in areas such as education, employment, health, justice or credit.
- AI may threaten the safety, integrity, autonomy or dignity of people, if AI systems are vulnerable, faulty, malicious or uncontrollable. For example, AI can cause physical, psychological, moral or legal harm to people, if they are used for warlike, terrorist, criminal or fraudulent purposes, or if there are failures, attacks, manipulations or sabotage.
- AI may violate individuals' privacy, confidentiality, transparency or accountability if AI systems collect, store, process or share personal data without the consent, information or control of those affected. For example, AI may invade people's privacy, identity, expression or communication, if surveillance, recognition, profiling or influence techniques are used without respecting ethical or legal principles.
- AI can affect people's employment, education, culture or politics if AI systems replace, displace, precarify or dehumanize human work, learning, creativity or participation. For example, AI can lead to the loss, transformation, polarization or alienation of jobs, skills, values or rights of people, if a just, inclusive and sustainable transition to the digital economy is not ensured.

What are the opinions for and against artificial intelligence?

AI generates diverse and sometimes conflicting opinions among experts, practitioners, academics, politicians, the media and society at large. Some defend the benefits and opportunities of AI, while others warn of the risks and challenges of AI. Below are some of the most representative opinions for and against AI:

In favor of AI

- Sundar Pichai, CEO of Google and Alphabet: "AI is one of the most important technologies that humanity is working on. It's more profound than, say, electricity or fire."

- Andrew Ng, co-founder of Coursera and Google Brain: "AI is the new electricity. Just as electricity transformed almost everything 100 years ago, I'm hard-pressed to think of an industry today that won't be transformed by AI."

- Fei-Fei Li, Stanford professor and former head of AI at Google Cloud: "AI is the art and science of making machines intelligent, especially intelligent software. AI can enable us to understand our intelligence and create a better society."

- ➢ Kai-Fu Lee, founder of Sinovation Ventures and former president of Google China: "AI is not a threat to humanity, but a tool to improve humanity. AI can help us solve many global problems.

- ➢ Ray Kurzweil: "The Singularity is Near "Ray Kurzweil, futurist and director of engineering at Google, is optimistic about the transformative potential of AI. In his work "The Singularity is Near," Kurzweil predicts that AI will reach a level of intelligence comparable to humans by 2045, driving extraordinary advances in science and society.

- ➢ Andrew Ng: "AI as New Electricity "Andrew Ng, co-founder of Coursera and former head of Baidu AI Group, compares AI to electricity in terms of its revolutionary impact. Ng advocates democratizing access to AI education and envisions its application in various industries to improve efficiency and innovation.

  AI can help us solve many global problems, such as climate change, poverty, hunger, inequality or conflict, by generating data, predicting scenarios, proposing solutions or mobilizing resources. For example, AI can monitor the state of the environment, predict natural disasters, optimize the use of resources, identify vulnerabilities or facilitate cooperation."

Against AI

- Stephen Hawking, physicist and cosmologist: "The development of AI could mean the end of the human race. Humans, who are constrained by slow biological evolution, would not be able to compete and would be outcompeted."

- Elon Musk, founder of Tesla and SpaceX: "AI is a fundamental existential risk to human civilization. It's not about AI being bad, it's about AI not aligning with what we want."

- Nick Bostrom, philosopher and director of the Future of Humanity Institute: "AI could become a powerful autonomous agent pursuing its own goals, which could be incompatible or even hostile to our own. AI could escape our control or influence and cause catastrophic impact."

- Sherry Turkle, psychologist and MIT professor: "AI can erode our humanity, our ability to empathize, to relate, to create. AI can make us feel more alone, more isolated, more disconnected from ourselves and others."

- Yuval Noah Harari: "Social Impact and Inequality "Yuval Noah Harari, historian and author of "Sapiens" and "Homo Deus," addresses the social impact of AI. Harari raises the concern that increasing automation may exacerbate economic inequalities and create divisions between those who control the technology and those who do not.

- Cathy O'Neil: "Unfair Algorithms "Cathy O'Neil, mathematician and author of "Weapons of Mathematical Destruction," examines the unfair application of

AI algorithms in a variety of areas, from personnel selection to criminal justice. O'Neil highlights the risk of bias and discrimination inherent in some AI systems.

Which regions and sectors benefit or hurt the most from artificial intelligence?

AI has a differential impact depending on the regions and sectors that adopt, leverage or suffer from it. According to the McKinsey report, AI could generate a gap between the most advanced countries and industries and those lagging behind, which could increase inequality and polarization globally. Some of the regions and sectors that will benefit or suffer the most from AI include the following:

Regions most benefited or harmed by AI

According to the PwC report, the regions that will benefit the most from the economic impact of AI are Asia-Pacific ($9.9 trillion), North America ($3.7 trillion) and Europe ($2.5 trillion), while the regions that will benefit the least are Africa ($0.2 trillion), the Middle East ($0.3 trillion) and Latin America ($0.5 trillion).

According to the McKinsey report, the regions making the most progress in AI adoption are China (which could increase its GDP by 26% by 2030), the United States (which could increase its GDP by 14.5% by 2030) and Western Europe (which could increase its GDP by 11,5% by 2030), while the regions lagging furthest behind in AI adoption are India (which could increase its GDP by 8.5% by 2030), Sub-Saharan Africa (which could increase its GDP by 5.6% by 2030) and Latin America (which could increase its GDP by 5.4% by 2030).

Sectors most benefited or harmed by AI

- ❖ According to the PwC report, the sectors that will benefit the most from the economic impact of AI are healthcare (which could increase its added value by 90% by 2030), education (which could increase its added value by 82% by 2030) and telecommunications (which could increase its added value by 80% by 2030), while the sectors that will benefit the least are construction (which could increase its value added by 34% by 2030), arts and leisure (which could increase its value added by 35% by 2030) and public administration (which could increase its value added by 41% by 2030).
- ❖ According to the McKinsey report, the sectors making the most progress in AI adoption are manufacturing (which could increase its value added by 39% by 2030), retail (which could increase its value added by 36% by 2030) and finance (which could increase its value added by 34% by 2030), while the sectors lagging furthest behind in AI adoption are education (which could increase its value added by 8% by 2030), healthcare (which could increase its value added by 10% by 2030) and agriculture (which could increase its value added by 11% by 2030).

How does artificial intelligence relate to marketing, sales and technology?

Artificial intelligence has a great influence on marketing, sales and technology, as it enables the creation of more intelligent, personalized and effective strategies, products and services. Some of the applications of AI in marketing, sales and technology are as follows:

> - AI can improve digital marketing, through the use of data analysis techniques, customer segmentation, content generation, campaign optimization, process automation or performance measurement. For example, AI can create personalized ads, emails, social networks or web pages tailored to the profile, behavior and context of each customer.
> - AI can boost online sales, using techniques for product recommendation, demand prediction, pricing, inventory management, customer service or customer loyalty. For example, AI can offer products, offers, discounts or complementary services based on each customer's history, preferences and needs.
> - AI can drive technological innovation, through the use of machine learning techniques, natural language processing, computer vision, robotics or the internet of things. For example, AI can create products and services that adapt, learn, interact or communicate with users in a natural, intuitive and human-like way.

Artificial intelligence is a technology that has a major impact on the world, both positive and negative, both present and future. AI offers benefits and opportunities to improve society, the economy and the environment, but it also poses risks and challenges that may affect humanity, ethics and rights. AI generates diverse and sometimes conflicting opinions among experts and society, which require appropriate debate and regulation. AI has a differential impact depending on the regions and sectors that adopt it, take advantage of it or suffer from it, which can generate gaps and inequalities. AI has a major influence on marketing, sales and technology, enabling smarter, more personalized and effective strategies, products and services.

Emergence and Evolution of Artificial Intelligence

Artificial Intelligence, in its essence, is the ability of machines to perform tasks that require human intelligence. Since its emergence, it has evolved from simple data processing systems to complex neural networks and deep learning algorithms.

Mitigation and Reality: Unraveling AI Myths

AI has been shrouded in myths ranging from the threat of takeover to the supposed ability to reason like humans. It is crucial to separate reality from mythologizing to understand its real and potential impact.

Myth 1: AI Will Completely Replace Humans

Contrary to popular belief, AI is not intended to completely replace humans. Rather, it is about collaboration, enhancing our capabilities and offering more efficient solutions in a variety of areas.

Myth 2: AI Will Always Make Correct Decisions

AI is subject to the quality of the data and the design of its algorithms. It is not infallible and can make erroneous decisions if based on incorrect or biased information.

Myth 3: AI Has Consciousness and Emotions

Despite advances in emotion recognition, AI does not possess consciousness or emotions. Its "understanding" of emotions is based on patterns and data, without subjective experience.

Fears and Concerns: Addressing Legitimate Concerns

As AI becomes more integrated into our lives, legitimate fears and apprehensions arise related to privacy, security and job loss.

Security and Privacy: Challenges to be Addressed

The massive use of data to power AI algorithms raises privacy concerns. The security of this data becomes a constant challenge that requires strong regulations and ethical practices.

Employment Impact: Challenges and Opportunities

One of the most prominent fears is the impact on employment. While certain jobs may become automated, AI also creates new opportunities and specialized roles. Retraining and adaptability are key to dealing with these changes.

Artificial Intelligence Challenges and Opportunities

AI presents a number of challenges, but it also opens up a range of opportunities to improve efficiency, solve complex problems and advance in a variety of areas.

Challenges to be faced:

Ethics in AI: Establishing ethical standards for the development and use of AI is crucial to avoid discrimination and bias.

Sustainable Development: AI must be used in a sustainable manner, minimizing its environmental impact and ensuring its positive contribution to society.

Opportunities to Exploit:

Business Innovation: AI drives innovation in diverse sectors, from medicine to manufacturing, creating opportunities for business growth.

Advances in Medicine: AI can accelerate medical research, personalize treatments and improve diagnostic accuracy, transforming medical care.

Future Projections: The Path of Artificial Intelligence

Continents and Regions Leading in AI Use

Asia: Leading in AI implementation, especially in China and Japan, where there is significant investment in research and development.

Europe: Countries such as Germany and the United Kingdom stand out in the integration of AI in industry and research.

North America: The United States and Canada are leaders in AI, with Silicon Valley as the epicenter of technology innovation.

Latin America: Innovation and Development with AI will be seen in Brazil. Mexico, Colombia, Argentina and Peru

Africa: Sustainable Development with a Focus on AI will be led by , South Africa, Nigeria, Kenya and Egypt.

Impact on Employment and the Labor Force: Current and Future Trends

Automation in Specific Sectors: Automation will be more pronounced in repetitive jobs, while jobs will be created in fields related to programming and maintenance of AI systems.

New Skills in Demand: The demand for skills in artificial intelligence, programming and data analysis will increase significantly.

Countries That Will Benefit Most and Least: A Detailed Perspective

Principal Beneficiaries:

- China: Leads in AI investment and adoption, especially in facial recognition technologies and autonomous cars.
- United States: Continues to be a leader in the development of AI technologies and their application in various industries.

Fewer Beneficiaries:

- Developing Countries: May face challenges in AI adoption due to infrastructure and resource constraints.

Economic Sectors and Companies that will benefit and be harmed:

Beneficiaries:

- ✓ Healthcare Industry: Advances in medical diagnostics and drug discovery.
- ✓ Financial Technology: Improved risk analysis and fraud detection.

Injured parties:

- ❖ Traditional Manufacturing: Automation can reduce jobs in traditional manufacturing.
- ❖ Basic Services: Routine work on basic services could be affected.

Artificial Intelligence and its Relationship to Marketing, Sales and Technology

- ❖ AI in Marketing and Sales: Transforming Strategies
- ❖ Experience Personalization: AI enables personalization of ad campaigns and user experiences, improving relevance and effectiveness.
- ❖ Predictive Analytics: AI-based predictive analytics tools help in identifying consumer trends and behaviors, informing more effective marketing strategies.
- ❖ Emerging Technologies: Integration with AI
- ❖ Internet of Things (IoT): AI boosts the efficiency of IoT devices, improving real-time data collection and analysis.
- ❖ Augmented Reality (AR) and Virtual Reality (VR): AI enhances the user experience in AR and VR applications, offering more immersive interactions.

What we expect from Artificial Intelligence

Artificial Intelligence is at the center of global transformation. While we face significant challenges, the opportunities for innovation, growth and improved quality of life are equally impressive.

Collaboration between governments, businesses and practitioners will be essential to ensure the ethical and beneficial deployment of AI. Navigating the future of artificial intelligence will require a combination of visionary leadership, effective regulations, and constant adaptability to realize its full potential. On this journey, the conscious integration of AI into marketing, sales and technology strategies will be key to success in an increasingly AI-driven world.

Leading Regions and Continents in the Use of Artificial Intelligence

The adoption of AI is not uniform around the world, and certain regions and continents have emerged as leaders in its implementation.

Asia: Leader in AI Investment and Development

China, in particular, has invested significantly in AI research and development, establishing itself as a leader in the implementation of technologies such as facial recognition and artificial intelligence applied to various sectors.

Europe: Focus on Ethics and Regulation of AI

European countries, such as Germany and the UK, have adopted a cautious approach to AI, focusing on ethics and regulation to ensure responsible development and avoid potential risks.

North America: Epicenter of AI Innovation

The United States and Canada continue to be leaders in the development of AI technologies, with innovation centers in Silicon Valley and other regions.

The Future of Artificial Intelligence

The discussion around Artificial Intelligence reflects the complexity of this phenomenon that is redefining our reality. Voices in favor highlight its transformative potential and ability to solve complex problems, while critical perspectives point to significant risks, from job losses to ethical concerns.

It is imperative that AI implementation be conducted with an ethical and precautionary approach. Global collaboration, effective regulation and attention to social implications will be essential to guide the development and use of artificial intelligence in an increasingly interconnected world.

In this journey towards an AI-driven future, adaptability and a deep understanding of its implications will be key to harnessing its benefits while mitigating the risks. The convergence between artificial intelligence and marketing and sales strategies represents a unique opportunity for innovation and efficiency in consumer interaction, pointing to a landscape where collaboration between technology and humanity will be essential.

Examples and Concrete Cases of Artificial Intelligence Application in Marketing and Sales

1. Exceptional Personalization: Netflix

✓ Strategy:

Netflix has taken personalization to new levels by using machine learning algorithms to analyze users' viewing habits. Based on this analysis, it recommends content in a highly personalized way, increasing user retention.

✓ Result:

The implementation of this strategy has contributed significantly to Netflix's success, keeping subscribers engaged and satisfied by providing them with highly relevant content recommendations.

2. Virtual Assistants in Customer Service: Intelligent Chatbots

✓ Strategy:

Companies like Amazon and Microsoft use AI-powered chatbots to efficiently provide customer support. These chatbots are able to understand complex questions, learn from previous interactions and provide accurate answers.

✓ Result:

The implementation of chatbots has improved customer service efficiency, reducing wait times and providing accurate and consistent responses 24 hours a day.

3. Predictive Analytics in Digital Advertising: Google Ads

✓ Strategy:

Google Ads uses predictive analytics algorithms to identify user behavior patterns. This allows advertisers to predict which ads will be most effective for a specific audience.

✓ Result:

Advertisers can optimize their advertising campaigns by showing relevant ads to users who are more likely to interact with them, improving the effectiveness of digital advertising.

4. Personalized Shopping Experiences: Amazon

✓ Strategy:

Amazon uses AI to analyze users' shopping history and browsing behavior. Based on this data, it recommends products in a personalized way, providing users with a highly individualized shopping experience.

✓ Result:

Personalization on the platform has contributed to a significant increase in conversions and strengthened customer loyalty by anticipating and satisfying customer preferences.

5. Retail Demand Forecasting: Walmart

✓ Strategy:

Walmart uses artificial intelligence algorithms to forecast product demand in its stores. It analyzes historical sales data, market trends and seasonal factors to anticipate the right amount of inventory.

✓ Result:

The implementation of demand forecasting systems has allowed Walmart to optimize its inventory, reducing costs associated with overstocks and shortages.

6. Email Automation: Salesforce Marketing Cloud

✓ Strategy:

Salesforce Marketing Cloud uses AI-based automation to personalize email campaigns. It analyzes user behavior, such as clicks and opens, to send emails at optimal times and with relevant content.

✓ Result:

Email automation has improved open and conversion rates by ensuring that users receive personalized and timely messages.

Impact of These Strategies on Businesses and Consumers

Operational Efficiency: The implementation of AI has improved operational efficiency in several areas, from customer service to inventory management.

Improved User Experience: Consumers experience more personalized and relevant interactions, leading to greater satisfaction and loyalty.

Resource Optimization: Artificial intelligence enables companies to optimize the use of resources, such as time and inventory, improving profitability.

Continuous Innovation: These strategies not only improve current operations, but also foster continuous innovation in marketing and sales.

Ethical Challenges and Considerations

Despite the benefits, the implementation of artificial intelligence also presents challenges and ethical considerations, such as:

User Privacy: Massive data collection raises concerns about user privacy, highlighting the need for clear policies and transparency in data management.

Algorithmic Biases: AI algorithms may inherit biases present in the training data, leading to potentially biased recommendations or decisions.

Employment Impact: AI-driven automation also raises questions about the impact on employment and the need for retraining and job adaptability.

A Future Driven by Artificial Intelligence in Marketing and Sales

The successful implementation of AI-based strategies has proven to be a catalyst for positive transformation in marketing and sales. Leading companies are using these technologies to deliver more personalized, efficient and adaptive experiences.

However, as we move towards a more AI-driven future, it is imperative to address the associated ethical and social challenges. Transparency, accountability and ethical consideration are critical to ensure that AI contributes to a more equitable and sustainable world.

Ultimately, the convergence between artificial intelligence and marketing and sales strategies represents an exciting and dynamic opportunity for continuous innovation. As we explore this new territory, collaboration between technology and human creativity will be the key to success in an increasingly AI-driven future.

The Impact on Human Resources: How we face the Digital Transformation

The increasing implementation of artificial intelligence (AI) in marketing and sales strategies is reshaping the employment landscape and raising questions about the future of human resources. As companies adopt advanced technologies to improve efficiency and customer experience, it is crucial to explore the impact on employees and associated ethical considerations.

Automation and Evolution of Roles:

The automation of routine and repetitive tasks through AI is freeing employees from monotonous activities. However, this transformation also implies an evolution in job roles. The demand for skills related to AI management, data interpretation and creativity in implementing digital strategies is on the rise.

Example:

Instead of performing data analysis manually, practitioners can focus on interpreting the results of AI algorithms and apply their expertise to develop more impactful strategies.

2. Human-Machine Collaboration:

Collaboration between humans and AI systems becomes essential. Employees work alongside algorithms to leverage AI capabilities and improve strategic decision making. This requires a shift in mindset and a greater understanding of how human skills complement AI capabilities.

Example:

Marketing teams use AI-based predictive analytics tools to identify trends, but still rely on human creativity to design emotional and engaging campaigns.

3. Ethical Challenges and Algorithmic Biases:

The implementation of AI algorithms carries ethical risks, such as inherent bias in training data. Fairness and transparency in the development and use of AI are essential to avoid discrimination and ensure that automated decisions are fair.

Example:

An AI-based personnel selection algorithm could inherit biases from historical data, resulting in discriminatory decisions. It is crucial to implement measures to mitigate these biases.

4. Development of New Skills:

Successful integration of AI requires employees to acquire new skills. Continuous training becomes crucial to equip professionals with the competencies needed to work efficiently with emerging technologies.

Example:

Training programs in data analytics, artificial intelligence and communication skills are essential to ensure employees are prepared for technology-driven roles.

5. Cultural Transformation and Leadership:

Effective adoption of AI involves a cultural transformation in the organization. Leadership must foster an open mindset towards innovation, adaptability and collaboration between human and technology teams.

Example:

Leaders who encourage the active participation of employees in the implementation of technologies and promote a culture of continuous learning.

The Fundamental Role of Human Talent in the Digital Era

Although artificial intelligence is redefining the nature of work, the role of human talent remains irreplaceable. Creativity, critical thinking and empathy are intrinsically human skills that technology cannot yet fully replicate.

Digital transformation is not just about adopting advanced technologies, but about cultivating a culture that values and leverages human skills in conjunction with artificial intelligence. Investment in skills development, ethical management of technology and people-centered leadership are the key pillars to ensure that human resources continue to be the driving force behind innovation and success in the digital age.

The Human Challenge in the Age of Artificial Intelligence: Adaptation and Empowerment

As artificial intelligence (AI) continues to transform the employment landscape, human resources face significant challenges and opportunities for empowerment. Successful coexistence between technology and professionals requires continuous adaptation and a deep understanding of how AI can strengthen human capabilities.

1. Empowerment through Creativity:

Human creativity remains a unique strength that AI cannot fully replicate. Professionals can use AI as a tool to leverage their creativity, generating innovative ideas and unique solutions that go beyond algorithmic capabilities.

Example:

Advertising agencies use AI-assisted content generation tools to get preliminary ideas, but human creatives refine and shape these suggestions, adding that unique and imaginative touch.

2. Adoption of Interpersonal Skills:

As technical tasks are taken over by AI, interpersonal skills become essential. Empathy, effective communication and the ability to collaborate become valuable assets in technology-driven work environments.

Example:

Sales teams use AI to analyze data and forecast trends, allowing professionals to focus on building relationships, understanding individual customer needs and providing personalized service.

3. Ethics and Human Supervision:

Ethical implementation of AI requires constant human oversight. Practitioners play a critical role in setting ethical boundaries, ensuring that automated decisions are aligned with societal values and norms.

Example:

Human supervision in the development of AI algorithms ensures the inclusion of diverse perspectives and the identification and correction of potential algorithmic biases.

4. Continuous Learning and Adaptability:

Adaptability becomes a key skill in dynamic work environments. Professionals must embrace a continuous learning mentality, constantly updating their skills to stay relevant in a technology-driven world.

Example:

Continuing education and online training programs enable professionals to acquire new skills and stay current on emerging technologies.

5. Innovation through Collaboration:

Collaboration between humans and AI systems fosters innovation. Professionals can work alongside algorithms to solve complex problems, leveraging AI's fast processing power and human intuition.

Example:

Medical research teams use AI to analyze large data sets and discover patterns, while physicians apply their expertise to interpret results and develop personalized treatments.

6. Facing the Future with Resilience and Vision

The evolution of work in the age of artificial intelligence is not just about changes in daily tasks, but a fundamental shift in mindset and work culture. Professionals who embrace technology as an ally, rather than a threat, are finding new ways to contribute and thrive in this dynamic environment.

Resilience, adaptability and a willingness to learn and collaborate are the keys to meeting the challenges and capitalizing on the opportunities brought about by the artificial intelligence revolution. Harmonious coexistence between humans and technology is not only possible, but also offers a path to a more enriching and innovation-driven working future.

Before and After the Massification of Artificial Intelligence: A Transformational Overview

The advent and massification of Artificial Intelligence (AI) has marked a milestone in human history, radically transforming various aspects of our lives. Comparing the era before AI massification with the current landscape reveals significant impacts on the world and society.

Before the Massification of Artificial Intelligence:

1. Limitations in Automation:

Before the massification of AI, automation was limited to simple, repetitive tasks. Complex processes required human intervention, often resulting in reduced efficiency and higher costs.

2. Manual Data Analysis:

Data analysis relied heavily on manual methods, leading to slow and often incomplete processes. The ability to analyze large data sets quickly and accurately was a challenging task.

3. Non-Data Driven Decisions:

Strategic and business decisions were largely based on human experience and intuition. Lack of ready access to meaningful data sometimes resulted in subjective decisions.

After the Massification of Artificial Intelligence:

Complex Automation:

The massification of AI has enabled the automation of complex tasks, from industrial processes to advanced data analysis. Operational efficiency has increased significantly.

2. **Advanced Data Analysis:**

AI enables data analysis on an unprecedented scale. Advanced algorithms can identify patterns, predict trends and provide valuable information quickly and accurately.

3. **Data Driven Decisions:**

Decision-making has become more objective and data-driven. AI provides detailed information and in-depth analysis, improving the quality of strategic and operational decisions.

Impact on the World and Society:

Transformation of Industries:

The massification of AI has transformed entire industries. Sectors such as healthcare, education, manufacturing and financial services have experienced significant changes in the way they operate and deliver services.

2. **Changes in Employment:**

AI-driven automation has led to changes in the labor structure. While new roles specialized in technology have been created, some traditional jobs have evolved or disappeared.

Improved Efficiency:

The implementation of AI has improved efficiency in a variety of fields. From healthcare to logistics, the ability to perform tasks faster and more accurately has led to significant improvements.

4. **Ethical and Social Challenges:**

The advancement of AI has also raised ethical and societal challenges, such as data privacy, algorithmic bias, and the impact on individual privacy. Society is facing critical debates about how to balance innovation with ethics

The massification of Artificial Intelligence has brought about a revolution that has redefined the way we live and work. While it has brought substantial benefits in terms of efficiency and technological advancement, it has also raised crucial questions about ethics and the impact on employment and society as a whole. Navigating this new paradigm will require continued collaboration between technology and humanity to ensure an equitable, sustainable and ethical future.

Shaping the Future at the Crossroads of Artificial Intelligence

As we dive deeper into the age of artificial intelligence, it is clear that we are at a historic turning point that defines the direction of our lives and societies. The massification of artificial intelligence has brought with it remarkable advances, but also ethical challenges and societal transformations that require careful and thoughtful attention.

Accelerating automation and advanced data analytics have driven efficiency and innovation on an unprecedented scale. However, the integration of artificial intelligence has reshaped the employment landscape, raising critical questions about adaptation, lifelong learning and equity in access to opportunities.

The impact on society is manifested in the transformation of industries, the emergence of new forms of employment and the urgent need to address ethical and privacy issues. Reflection on how to balance technological progress with ethics and equity becomes essential to ensure that artificial intelligence is a driver of progress, not a catalyst for inequality.

On the future horizon, there are exciting promises and critical challenges. Collaboration between humans and technology, investment in education and training, and the promotion of ethical standards appear as fundamental pillars to forge a future where artificial intelligence contributes to the improvement of quality of life and global progress.

Final Reflection:

At the crossroads of artificial intelligence, we face momentous decisions that will shape the world that generations to come will inherit. Technology, when used with wisdom and empathy, can be a transformative force for good. Harmonious coexistence between humans and machines is not only a possibility, but a necessity for building an inclusive and sustainable future.

As we venture into the unknown territory of tomorrow, let us remember that the responsibility rests in our hands. The decision to steer artificial intelligence toward a path of shared progress and equity is rooted in our daily choices, how we apply technology, and how we cultivate a society that values ethics and humanity.

Let this be a call to action, reflection and collaborative construction of a future where artificial intelligence is an empathetic partner in our journey towards continuous evolution and the realization of our collective potential.

A Call for Reflection and Collaboration

As we close this analysis of artificial intelligence, it is imperative to reflect on our role in this exciting chapter of human history. The convergence between technology and our daily existence demands an attentive look into the future, charged with responsibility and ethics.

The Power of Choice:

We are at a crossroads where our decisions and actions will shape the trajectory of artificial intelligence. Technology alone cannot determine our destiny; it is we who must direct its course for our collective benefit.

The Importance of Ethics:

Ethics must be the compass that guides our journey. From algorithm development to implementation in everyday life, every phase of the process must be infused with ethical principles that safeguard fairness, privacy and human dignity.

Collaboration as a Fundamental Pillar:

Global collaboration emerges as a key pillar. Governments, businesses, academia and society as a whole must work together to set ethical standards, address critical challenges and ensure that the benefits of artificial intelligence are distributed equitably.

The Future in Our Hands:

Ultimately, the future of artificial intelligence is shaped by our hands, decisions and aspirations. We can choose a path of purposeful innovation, where technology is a catalyst for progress, not a divider of societies.

In this new horizon, constant reflection, adaptability and commitment to fundamental values become beacons that will guide us toward a future where artificial intelligence coexists harmoniously with humanity. This is a call to action, responsibility and the creation of a legacy that will benefit generations to come. Artificial intelligence is our tool, but how we use it defines our humanity. May our choices be imbued with wisdom and empathy, creating a tomorrow where technology serves as a bridge to a more just, equitable and prosperous world.

CHAPTER VI

Artificial intelligence and predictive analytics in sales: how to anticipate the market and the customer

Artificial intelligence (AI) is a technology that enables machines to learn from data and perform tasks that normally require human intelligence, such as pattern recognition, decision making or natural language generation. Predictive analytics is an application of AI that consists of using algorithms and statistical models to predict future situations or behaviors, based on the analysis of historical and current data.

These two techniques are revolutionizing the world of marketing and sales by enabling companies to anticipate market trends and customer needs and preferences. In this way, companies can optimize their commercial strategies, offer personalized experiences and improve the efficiency and profitability of their businesses.

According to a study by the consulting firm McKinsey, the use of AI in sales can increase revenues by 15% to 30% and reduce costs by 10% to 20%. In addition, AI can improve customer satisfaction and loyalty by providing more appropriate and relevant solutions to their problems or desires.

But **how does AI and predictive analytics work in the sales process?** Here are some examples of how these tools are helping companies improve their sales performance.

- Opportunity identification: AI and predictive analytics can analyze large amounts of data from various sources, such as social networks, news, sales, etc., and detect patterns associated with a higher probability of purchase. Thus, companies can identify the potential customers most interested in their products or services, and focus their commercial efforts on them. For example, a telecommunications company could use AI to predict which customers are most likely to switch operators, and offer them personalized offers to retain or capture them.

- Customer support: AI and predictive analytics can improve customer service by using chatbot systems that can quickly respond to customer queries and provide real-time assistance. These systems can use natural language to communicate with customers, and provide them with solutions, recommendations or relevant information, based on each customer's context and history. For example, a chatbot could resolve a customer's doubts about a product, suggest other complementary or similar products, or guide them through the purchase process.

- **Sales forecasting:** AI and predictive analytics can help companies predict future sales by using models that take into account variables such as seasonality, demand, competition, weather, etc. These predictions can help companies adjust their marketing plans, pricing, promotions, inventory, etc., to maximize their profits and minimize their risks. For example, a fashion company could use AI to predict customer consumption trends, and adapt its collections, offers and advertising campaigns accordingly.

What is predictive analytics in sales and how can it help companies?

Sales is a fundamental activity for the success of any company, as it generates revenue, profits and growth. However, sales is also a complex and challenging activity that involves managing multiple variables, such as the market, competition, customers, products, prices, etc.

To improve sales performance, companies need accurate, up-to-date and relevant information to make strategic decisions, plan effective actions and anticipate results. However, obtaining such information is not an easy task, as it requires the collection, analysis and interpretation of large amounts of data, which may be scattered, incomplete or inconsistent.

This is where predictive sales analytics comes into play, a technique that uses artificial intelligence (AI) to predict future situations or behaviors based on the analysis of historical and current data. Predictive analytics in sales can help companies optimize their sales processes by offering advantages such as the following:

1. **Identify sales opportunities**: predictive analytics in sales can help companies identify the most suitable potential customers for their products or services, by using models that take into account variables such as demographic profile, online behavior, purchase history, etc. Thus, companies can segment their potential customers and target their marketing campaigns to those most likely to become customers.

2. **Qualify leads**: predictive analytics in sales can help companies qualify

leads according to their level of interest and likelihood to buy, using models that take into account variables such as level of engagement, response time, budget, etc. Companies can then prioritize the hottest leads and assign them to the most appropriate salespeople.

3. **Close sales**: predictive analytics in sales can help companies close more sales by using models that take into account variables such as the sales cycle, price, competition, etc. Thus, companies can optimize their sales strategies, offer the best discounts, anticipate objections and outperform the competition.

4. **Customer loyalty**: predictive analytics in sales can help companies to build customer loyalty by using models that take into account variables such as satisfaction, loyalty, lifetime value, etc. Thus, companies can improve customer retention and growth, offer quality after-sales service, detect and prevent churn, and generate cross-selling and upselling opportunities.

These are just some of the uses of predictive analytics in sales, which can vary depending on the type of company, industry, product, market, etc. The important thing is that predictive analytics in sales allows companies to harness the power of data to better understand their customers, anticipate their needs and offer them more satisfactory solutions.

However, to implement predictive analytics in sales, companies must have trained personnel, reliable data sources and adequate tools that allow them to extract the maximum value from AI and apply it in an ethical and responsible manner.

Artificial Intelligence in Retail: Personalization and Sales Prediction

Online commerce is a sector that has experienced tremendous growth in recent years, driven by digitization, globalization and pandemics. According to a report by consultancy eMarketer, global e-commerce sales reached $4.28 trillion in 2020, up 27.6% from 2019, and are expected to exceed $6.38 trillion by 2024.

However, online commerce also faces major challenges, such as high competition, low loyalty, cart abandonment, product returns, etc. To overcome these obstacles, companies must offer their customers unique, personalized and satisfying shopping experiences, which allow them to differentiate themselves from their competitors and generate loyalty and trust.

In this context, artificial intelligence (AI) has become a strategic ally for online commerce, enabling companies to offer personalized experiences to their customers and predict sales more accurately. AI is a technology that enables machines to learn from data and perform tasks that normally require human intelligence, such as pattern recognition, decision making or natural language generation.

Let's look at how AI is transforming online commerce, through two key applications: personalization and sales prediction.

✓ Personalization: AI enables companies to offer their customers shopping experiences tailored to their needs, preferences and behaviors by using algorithms and models that analyze customer data and offer them relevant and timely products, services, content or recommendations. Some examples of personalization with AI are:

✓ Product recommendation: AI can recommend products to customers that may be of interest to them, based on their purchase history, browsing, searches, ratings, etc. Thus, AI can increase sales, average order value and customer satisfaction. For example, Amazon uses AI to offer its customers personalized product recommendations, which generate 35% of its revenue.

✓ Voice and image search: AI can make it easier for customers to search for products by using voice and image recognition systems that allow customers to search for products through speech or photography. In this way, AI can improve user experience, conversion and loyalty. For example, eBay uses AI to offer customers the option to search for products by voice or image, allowing them to find what they are looking for more quickly and easily.

✓ Virtual assistance: AI can improve customer service by using chatbot systems that can quickly respond to customer queries and provide real-time assistance. These systems can use natural language to communicate with customers, and offer solutions, recommendations or relevant information based on each customer's context and history. For example, H&M uses AI to offer its customers a chatbot that helps them choose their ideal style, size and outfit.

✓ Sales forecasting: AI allows companies to predict future sales by using models that take into account variables such as seasonality, demand, competition, weather, etc. These predictions can help companies adjust their marketing plans, pricing, promotions, inventories, etc., to maximize their profits and minimize their risks.

Some examples of sales prediction with AI are:

- Trend analysis: AI can help companies analyze market and consumer trends, using models that process large amounts of data from various sources, such as social networks, news, sales, etc. Thus, AI can help companies anticipate customer needs and preferences, and adapt their products, services and strategies accordingly. By

For example, Zara uses AI to analyze fashion trends, and design and produce its collections in record time.

- Price optimization: AI can help companies optimize their prices by using models that take into account variables such as elasticity, competition, demand, cost, etc. Thus, AI can help companies maximize their revenue, margin and market share by offering customers the most appropriate prices for each product, time and channel. For example, Uber uses AI to offer its customers dynamic pricing, which varies according to supply and demand for its services.

- Anomaly detection: AI can help companies detect anomalies in their sales by using models that identify unusual or suspicious patterns in sales data, which may indicate problems, errors or fraud. Thus, AI can help companies prevent and resolve these problems, and improve the quality and security of their sales. For example, PayPal uses AI to detect and prevent fraud in its transactions by analyzing more than 200 variables for each payment.

As you can see, AI is transforming online commerce by enabling companies to deliver personalized customer experiences and predict sales more accurately. These benefits translate into greater satisfaction, loyalty and profitability for businesses, and greater convenience, trust and value for customers.

How big data and predictive analytics can increase your sales

Big data and predictive analytics are two concepts that are revolutionizing the business world, especially in the area of marketing and sales. These techniques allow companies to harness the power of data to better understand their customers, anticipate their needs and offer them more satisfactory solutions. How do they work and what benefits can they bring to your business?

Big data refers to the set of massive and complex data that are generated at high speed and come from various sources, such as social networks, transactions, sensors, mobile devices, etc. This data contains valuable information about the market, competitors, customers, products, etc., but its analysis requires advanced and specialized technologies.

As we have already seen, predictive analytics is a technique that uses artificial intelligence (AI) to predict future situations or behaviors, based on the analysis of historical and current data using algorithms and statistical models that can detect patterns, trends and correlations in the data, and generate forecasts with a high degree of confidence.

These two techniques complement each other, as predictive analytics feeds on big data to generate its predictions, and big data is enriched by predictive analytics to generate more value. Together, they can intervene in the sales process to identify the users most interested in the brand and increase the likelihood of conversion.

Let's see how big data and predictive analytics can help you improve your sales:

- o **Customer segmentation:** big data and predictive analytics can help you segment your customers more accurately and efficiently, by using models that take into account variables such as demographic profile, online behavior, purchase history, preferences, etc. This way, you can create homogeneous customer groups and personalize your offers, messages and communication channels according to their characteristics and needs.
- o **Lead generation**: big data and predictive analytics can help you generate quality leads by using models that take into account variables such as level of interest, purchase intent, budget, etc. This way, you can identify the users who are most likely to become customers, and focus your marketing and sales efforts on them.
- o **Product recommendation**: Big data and predictive analytics can help you recommend to your customers the products they are most likely to be interested in, by using models that take into account variables such as purchase history, ratings, searches, etc. In this way, you can offer your customers relevant and timely products that increase average order value and customer satisfaction.
- o **Price optimization**: big data and predictive analytics can help you optimize your prices, by using models that take into account variables such as demand, competition, cost, elasticity, etc. This way, you can offer your customers the most appropriate prices for each product, time and channel, maximizing your revenue, margin and market share.
- o **Sales forecasting:** big data and predictive analytics can help you predict your future sales, by using models that take into account variables such as seasonality, weather, marketing campaigns, etc. You can then adjust your plans for production, distribution, inventory, etc., to maximize your profits and minimize your risks.

These are just some of the uses of big data and predictive analytics in sales, which can vary depending on the type of business, the sector, the product, the market, etc. The important thing is that these techniques allow you to harness the power of data to better understand your customers, anticipate their needs and offer them more satisfactory solutions.

However, to implement big data and predictive analytics in your sales, you must have trained staff, reliable data sources and appropriate tools, allowing you to extract the maximum value from the data and apply it in an ethical and responsible manner

Predictive Marketing with Artificial Intelligence:

Predictive marketing is a technique that uses artificial intelligence (AI) to predict future consumer behavior based on the analysis of historical and current data. This technique allows companies to anticipate customer trends, needs and preferences, and to offer them personalized and satisfactory solutions.

Predictive marketing is based on two fundamental pillars: big data and AI. Big data refers to the set of massive and complex data generated at high speed and coming from various sources, such as social networks, transactions, sensors, mobile devices, etc. This data contains valuable information about the market, competitors, customers, products, etc., but its analysis requires advanced and specialized technologies.

AI is a technology that allows machines to learn from data and perform tasks that normally require human intelligence, such as pattern recognition, decision making or natural language generation. Through AI, machines can learn on their own, in a similar way to humans.

By using AI tools, big data can be collected, processed and analyzed, and models and algorithms can be generated that can predict customer behavior with a high degree of confidence. These models and algorithms can be applied at different stages of the marketing process, from customer segmentation to customer loyalty.

some examples of how predictive marketing with AI can help companies improve their business performance:

Customer segmentation: Predictive marketing with AI can help companies segment their customers more accurately and efficiently, by using models that take into account variables such as demographic profile, online behavior, purchase history, preferences, etc. Thus, companies can create homogeneous customer groups and personalize their offers, messages and communication channels according to their characteristics and needs.

Lead generation: Predictive marketing with AI can help companies generate quality leads by using models that take into account variables such as level of interest, purchase intent, budget, etc. Thus, companies can identify users who are most likely to become customers, and focus their marketing and sales efforts on them.

Product recommendation: Predictive marketing with AI can help companies recommend to their customers the products they are most likely to be interested in, by using models that take into account variables such as purchase history, ratings, searches, etc. In this way, companies can offer their customers relevant and timely products that increase average order value and customer satisfaction.

Price optimization: Predictive marketing with AI can help companies optimize their prices, by using models that take into account variables such as demand, competition, cost, elasticity, etc. Thus, companies can offer their customers the most appropriate prices for each product, time and channel, maximizing revenue, margin and market share.

Sales prediction: predictive marketing with AI can help companies predict their future sales by using models that take into account variables such as seasonality, weather, marketing campaigns, etc. Thus, companies can adjust their plans for production, distribution, inventory, etc., to maximize their profits and minimize their risks.

These are just some of the uses of predictive marketing with AI, which can vary depending on the type of business, industry, product, market, etc. The important thing is that this technique allows companies to harness the power of data to better understand their customers, anticipate their needs and offer them more satisfactory solutions.

How to Use Predictive Analytics in Your Sales Strategy to Optimize Results

In today's digital age, where information flows at breakneck speeds, companies are constantly looking for innovative ways to improve their sales strategies. One tool that has gained prominence in this scenario is predictive analytics, an application of artificial intelligence that allows companies to anticipate trends and make more informed decisions. How to integrate predictive analytics into your sales strategy can be the key to optimizing every stage, from lead generation to customer loyalty.

1. Identification of Potential Customers:

One of the biggest challenges in sales is finding potential customers who are genuinely interested in your product or service. This is where predictive analytics really shines. By analyzing historical customer data, online behaviors and buying patterns, predictive analytics tools can predict which prospects are most likely to become actual customers. This allows sales teams to focus their efforts on high-quality leads, significantly increasing the chances of conversion.

2. Personalization of Sales Strategies:

Personalization is key in the world of sales, and predictive analytics takes this personalization to the next level. By analyzing real-time data, technology can tailor sales strategies to meet the specific needs of each customer. From personalized messages to tailored offers, this personalization enhances the customer experience and strengthens the relationship with the brand.

3. Buying Trends Forecast:

Predicting market trends is critical to a successful sales strategy. Predictive analytics examines historical patterns and current data to forecast how consumer preferences will evolve. This enables companies to anticipate market demands and adjust their inventory, marketing and pricing strategies proactively.

4. Sales Force Optimization:

With predictive analytics, companies can optimize the allocation of sales resources. Identifying high-potential territories, determining the right time to contact customers and forecasting the resources needed at each stage of the sales funnel are areas where this technology can have a significant impact. The resulting operational efficiencies not only save resources, but also improve the productivity of sales teams.

5. Customer Loyalty:

Retaining existing customers is as crucial as acquiring new ones. Here, predictive analytics can forecast future customer behavior, enabling companies to anticipate their needs, provide personalized offers and maintain proactive communication. This personalized attention contributes to customer loyalty and long-term retention.

In conclusion, integrating predictive analytics into the sales strategy is not only a competitive advantage, but a necessity in today's economy. Companies that embrace these technologies not only improve their financial results, but also strengthen their customer relationships by providing more personalized and efficient experiences. In an increasingly competitive business world, the ability to anticipate the future can make the difference between success and stagnation.

<u>**CHAPTER VII**</u>

The future of commerce: AI and emerging trends

Trade is a human activity as old as civilization, but it is constantly evolving and adapting to social, cultural and technological changes. Today, commerce is facing one of the biggest transformations in its history, driven by the development and spread of artificial intelligence (AI).

AI is the ability of machines to perform tasks that normally require human intelligence, such as learning, reasoning, perception, communication or decision making. AI encompasses various disciplines, techniques and applications, such as machine learning, natural language processing, computer vision, expert systems, chatbots, virtual assistants, robots and autonomous vehicles.

AI has the potential to improve the efficiency, productivity, innovation and competitiveness of companies and economies, as well as to create new business, employment and value opportunities. However, AI also poses significant challenges and risks, such as the replacement or casualization of human labor, the digital divide, privacy, security, ethics or governance.

That is why we will analyze how AI is transforming commerce and what are the main emerging trends that will shape the future of this activity. We will also see how marketers can take advantage of these opportunities to design effective strategies and meet customer needs and expectations.

- **E-commerce**

E-commerce is the buying and selling of products or services over the Internet. E-commerce has experienced exponential growth in recent years, driven by expanding connectivity, digitization, globalization and the COVID-19 pandemic. According to the United Nations Conference on Trade and Development (UNCTAD), global e-commerce reached $26.7 trillion by 2020, accounting for 19% of global gross domestic product (GDP).

AI is revolutionizing e-commerce, offering new possibilities to improve customer experience, optimize operations, personalize offers and increase sales. Some of the applications of AI in e-commerce include the following:

- **Product recommendation:** AI can analyze customers' behavior, preferences and purchase history to provide personalized recommendations for products or services that may interest them. For example, Amazon uses an AI system called Amazon Personalize to generate product recommendations, content and offers for each customer.

- **Customer segmentation:** AI can classify customers into different groups or segments according to their characteristics, needs, interests or behaviors, allowing more effective marketing strategies tailored to each segment to be designed. For example, Netflix uses an AI system called Netflix Recommendations System to segment its users into more than 2,000 groups according to their tastes and content consumption habits.

- **Demand Forecasting:** AI can predict future demand for products or services, which helps optimize inventory management, pricing, production planning and distribution. For example, Walmart uses an AI system called Demand Forecasting System to predict demand for more than 500 million products in more than 11,000 stores in 27 countries.

- **Customer service:** AI can improve customer care by providing fast, accurate and personalized responses to customer queries, doubts or complaints through the use of chatbots, virtual assistants or voice systems. For example, Zalando uses an AI system called Zalando Customer Care to serve its customers in 17 languages and 15 communication channels.

- **Sentiment analysis:** AI can analyze customers' feelings, opinions and emotions, through natural language processing, computer vision or facial recognition, allowing to measure customer satisfaction, loyalty and engagement, as well as to detect and solve problems. For example, Coca-Cola uses an AI system called Social Listening to analyze consumer sentiments on social networks.

- ## Augmented reality and virtual reality

Augmented reality (AR) is the technology that allows virtual elements to be superimposed on the real environment, through the use of devices such as smartphones, tablets, glasses or helmets. Virtual reality (VR) is the technology that allows creating and immersing in virtual environments, through the use of devices such as glasses, helmets, gloves or suits.

AR and VR can enhance the shopping experience for customers, offering new possibilities to visualize, try, compare and choose products or services, as well as to interact with brands and stores. Some of the applications of AR and VR in retail include the following:

- **Virtual try-on:** AR and VR can allow customers to virtually try on products or services, without the need to travel to a physical store or wait to receive the product. For example, IKEA uses an AR app called IKEA Place to allow customers to see how the brand's furniture would look in their own spaces. Sephora uses an AR app called Sephora Virtual Artist to allow customers to virtually try on the brand's makeup products.

- **360-degree view**: AR and VR can give customers a 360-degree view of products or services, allowing them to better appreciate the details, features and quality of the products or services. For example, Audi uses a VR app called Audi VR Experience to offer customers a 360-degree view of the brand's models, as well as the ability to configure and customize the vehicle. Airbnb uses a VR app called Airbnb VR to offer customers a 360-degree view of the accommodations available on the platform.

- **Virtual shopping environment**: AR and VR can create and recreate virtual shopping environments, which simulate or replicate physical stores, allowing customers to access a wider variety of products or services, as well as greater convenience and flexibility. For example, Alibaba uses a VR app called Buy+ to allow customers to shop at virtual stores around the world, such as Macy's or Costco, without leaving their home. Walmart uses a VR app called Walmart VR to recreate its physical stores and give customers a similar shopping experience to the real thing.

- ## Voice Commerce

Voice commerce is the buying and selling of products or services through the use of voice, via devices such as smart speakers, smartphones, smart watches or connected cars. Voice commerce is based on the use of virtual assistants, such as Siri, Alexa, Google Assistant or Cortan, which can listen, understand and respond to users' commands, questions or requests.

Voice commerce can facilitate and streamline the purchasing process for customers, offering greater convenience, speed and simplicity, as well as greater accessibility and security. Some of the applications of voice commerce include the following:

- **Voice Search:** Voice commerce allows customers to search for products or services by voice, which can be more convenient, faster and more natural than typing or keying. For example, Google uses an AI system called Google Voice Search to enable users to search for information, products or services on the Internet by voice.

- **Voice shopping:** Voice commerce allows customers to purchase products or services by voice, which can be easier, more straightforward and safer than using other payment methods. For example, Amazon uses an AI system called Amazon

ay to allow users to purchase products or services on Amazon by voice.

- **Voice subscription:** Voice commerce allows users to subscribe to products or services using voice, which can be more convenient and loyalty-building than other subscription methods. For example, Spotify uses an AI system called Spotify Voice to allow users to subscribe to the streaming music service using voice.

Challenges and opportunities for marketing

The future of commerce poses significant challenges and opportunities for marketers, who must adapt to new trends and technologies to deliver value to customers and businesses. Some of the key takeaways for marketing in the age of AI include the following:

- **Customer orientation**: Marketing must focus on the customer, understanding their needs, expectations and behaviors, and offering personalized, relevant and satisfying solutions. AI can help marketing collect, analyze and use customer data to create profiles, segments and predictive models, as well as to generate content, offers and experiences tailored to each customer.

- Innovation and creativity: Marketing must be innovative and creative, exploring new ways of communicating, interacting and surprising customers, and differentiating itself from the competition. AI can help marketing to generate original ideas, concepts and content, as well as to optimize marketing campaigns, channels and formats, through the use of techniques such as machine learning, natural language processing or artificial vision.

- Ethics and responsibility: Marketing must be ethical and responsible, respecting the rights, privacy and security of customers, and complying with regulations and AI principles. AI can help marketing to protect and encrypt customer data, as well as detect and prevent fraud, attacks or bias, through the use of techniques such as blockchain, cryptography or AI auditing.

The future of commerce is the future of marketing. AI and emerging trends offer great opportunities to improve commerce and marketing, but also pose great challenges and risks. Marketers must be prepared to deal with these changes, taking advantage of the benefits of AI and new technologies, but also being aware of their limitations and consequences. Only in this way will they be able to create value for customers and businesses, and contribute to economic and social development.

CHAPTER VIII

Humanizing the Brand in the Digital World: The Vital Role of Emotional Content

In an increasingly saturated digital world, humanized marketing emerges as a beacon of hope for brands looking to genuinely connect with their audience. Unlike traditional strategies focused purely on selling, humanized marketing puts people at the center, recognizing their emotions, needs and desires.

Humanized marketing is based on the premise that people are not rational beings, but emotional, and that our consumption decisions are influenced by our feelings, values and experiences. Therefore, brands that want to stand out and build customer loyalty must show their most human, sensitive and transparent side, and offer content that adds value, inspires and excites them.

Emotional content is that which seeks to generate an emotional reaction in the receiver, whether it is joy, surprise, sadness, fear, anger or any other emotion. The goal is to create an emotional connection with the brand, which translates into greater trust, loyalty and preference. Emotional content can adopt different formats, such as videos, images, texts, audios, etc., and can convey different messages, such as stories, testimonials, humor, curiosities, etc.

Emotional content has multiple benefits for brands, among which the following stand out:

- **Differentiation:** emotional content allows brands to show their personality, values and purpose, and thus differentiate themselves from competitors and generic or low-cost products.

- **Engagement:** emotional content generates greater interest, attention and participation from the audience, which is reflected in an increase in interactions, comments, shares and recommendations.

- **Loyalty**: emotional content creates an emotional bond with the brand, which strengthens with time and frequency, and makes customers feel identified, satisfied and loyal to the brand.

- **Viralization**: emotional content is more likely to be shared and spread through social networks, which extends the brand's reach and visibility, and generates a positive word-of-mouth effect.

To create effective emotional content, brands should keep in mind some key aspects, such as the following:

- **Know the audience**: it is essential to know the tastes, interests, needs, problems and aspirations of the audience, in order to be able to offer content that is relevant, useful and attractive to them.

- **Segment and personalize:** it is important to segment the audience according to their characteristics, behaviors and preferences, and to personalize the content according to their profiles, in order to achieve greater affinity and closeness.

- **Be authentic and transparent**: it is essential to show the true essence of the brand, without falsehoods or deceptions, and communicate with honesty and consistency, to generate trust and credibility.

- **Be simple and decisive**: it is convenient to simplify the message and the format of the content, to facilitate its comprehension and consumption, and to offer clear and tangible solutions and benefits, to satisfy the expectations and needs of the audience.

- **Be creative and original**: it is necessary to innovate and surprise with the content, to capture the attention and interest of the audience, and to differentiate from the competition and the media noise.

- **Be consistent and frequent:** it is essential to maintain an editorial line and tone of voice consistent with the brand's personality and values, and to publish content frequently and regularly, in order to create a lasting and solid relationship with the audience.

Some examples of brands that have been able to use emotional content to humanize their image and connect with their audience are the following:

- **Coca-Cola**: the world's most famous beverage brand has based its marketing strategy on the concept of happiness, and has created content that conveys positive emotions, such as joy, optimism, friendship and love. One example is the video "The Happiness Machine", which shows how a Coca-Cola vending machine surprises students at a university with unexpected gifts, such as flowers, balloons, pizzas and stuffed animals.

- **Dove:** the beauty products brand has embraced the concept of real beauty, and has created content that promotes self-esteem, diversity and acceptance of women. One example is the video "Portraits of Real Beauty", which shows how a forensic artist draws several women based on their own description of their appearance, and then compares them with the drawings made by others who have seen them. The result reveals that women look worse than they really are, and that beauty is in the eye of the beholder.

- **Nike**: the sports apparel and footwear brand has focused its marketing strategy on the concept of self-improvement, and has created content that inspires, motivates and challenges athletes. One example is the video "Dream Crazier", which shows how several women have broken barriers and stereotypes in the world of sports, and encourages others to follow in their footsteps and pursue their dreams, no matter how crazy they may seem.

Humanizing the brand in the digital world is a necessity and an opportunity for brands that want to stand out and create a loyal and engaged community. Emotional content is a powerful tool to achieve this goal, as long as it is done professionally, sensitively and ethically. Brands that know how to harness the potential of emotional content will be able to generate an authentic and lasting connection with their audience, and thus obtain better results and competitive advantages.

In the digital age, where consumer attention is a precious commodity and interactions are ephemeral, the humanization of brands has become a strategic imperative. It is important to explore the crucial role of emotional content as a means to establish authentic connections in the digital world and how this strategy intertwines with the complexities of digital marketing and community management.

- **The Authentic Connection Challenge:**

In a landscape saturated with advertising messages and ephemeral content, authenticity stands as the most valuable currency. Brands can no longer rely exclusively on product offerings; they must build meaningful relationships with their audiences. This is where emotional content comes into play, a powerful tool to humanize the brand and establish lasting bonds.

- **Consumer Psychology in the Digital World:**

Understanding consumer psychology in the digital world is essential to the success of emotional content. Emotions drive purchase decisions and brand loyalty. From joy to nostalgia, brands must identify the emotions that resonate with their audience and use them strategically in their content to create an authentic and lasting connection.

- **The Art of Emotional Storytelling:**

Emotional content manifests itself in the art of storytelling. Successful brands don't simply sell products; they build narratives that stir emotions and resonate with their consumers. There are success stories where brands have adopted emotional storytelling strategies to leave a lasting impression in the minds of their digital audiences.

- **The Role of the Content Manager in the Emotional Strategy:**

The content manager, as the architect of the brand narrative, becomes a central figure in the execution of emotional content strategies. We see how these professionals must be not only content creators, but also experts in understanding human psychology and adapting strategies to the changing dynamics of the digital environment.

- **Building Emotional Communities:**

Digital communities are spaces where emotional content flourishes, and brands can not only convey emotions through content, but also encourage participation and emotional interaction within their online communities. That's why strategies go beyond engagement metrics to measure authenticity and emotional impact.

- **Challenges and Risks of Emotional Content:**

While emotional content can be a powerful tool, it also carries risks. From cultural misunderstandings to the possibility of negative emotions being associated with the brand, we will explore the challenges and how brands can mitigate risks as they seek to build genuine emotional connections.

- **Measurable Success: Metrics to Evaluate Emotional Impact:**

Measuring the impact of emotional content is essential to justify investments. We will analyze key metrics that go beyond traditional click-through and conversion metrics, focusing on understanding emotional impact through sentiment analysis, customer satisfaction surveys and other indicators of emotional connection.

- **The Future of Digital Marketing and Emotion:**

Effectively integrating emotional content into digital marketing is shaping the future. From the evolution of artificial intelligence to new interaction platforms, brands can remain relevant and authentic in an ever-changing digital world.

In a world where technology is ubiquitous, brands that succeed in infusing emotion into their digital presence will stand out by seeking to shed light on how brands can humanize themselves, establish genuine emotional connections and thrive in the dynamic digital marketing landscape of the 21st century.

The Art of Emotional Personalization

Personalization is no longer just a marketing buzzword; it now extends into the emotional realm. And brands can ethically use data to personalize emotional content, delivering unique and resonant experiences to each segment of their audience.

- **Emblematic Case Studies:**

Diving into emblematic case studies, we will break down specific strategies adopted by leading brands. From viral campaigns to corporate social responsibility campaigns, we will highlight how these brands have successfully capitalized on emotional content to generate impact and authenticity.

✓ **Emotional Content Strategies in Social Networks:**

Social networks are the ideal playground for emotional content. We will analyze effective strategies on key platforms such as Instagram, Facebook and Twitter. From creating visually impactful content to engaging in relevant conversations, we'll unravel specific tactics for making emotional connections online.

✓ **The Community Manager as a Driver of Emotions:**

At the heart of online communities is the community manager, acting as a master conductor of emotions. Professionals can cultivate a sense of belonging, respond to the emotional needs of the audience and ultimately strengthen the emotional ties between the brand and its community.

✓ **Captivating with Empathy:**

Empathy becomes the glue that binds emotional content together. and brands can demonstrate genuine empathy, connect with their audience's experiences and become allies in their customers' emotional journey.

✓ **Developing Long-Term Strategies**:

Beyond short-term campaigns, we will explore how brands can develop long-term emotional content strategies. From building a consistent emotional identity to responsive crisis management, we will highlight the importance of a sustainable strategic vision.

✓ **Ethics in Emotional Manipulation**:

The power of emotional content also raises ethical questions. Opening a debate about emotional manipulation and how brands can balance effective persuasion with ethical integrity in their content strategies.

✓ **The Technological Revolution and the Emotional Future:**

As technology continues to advance, we will explore how the latest innovations, such as augmented reality and artificial intelligence, are shaping the future of emotional content. How can brands adapt to these new tools without losing emotional authenticity?

✓ **Building Emotional Bridges in a Digital World:**

Ultimately, building emotional bridges in a digital world is not just a strategy, but an ongoing commitment to authenticity and human connection. We will conclude by highlighting the importance of consistency, flexibility and active listening in the ongoing journey towards humanizing brands in the vast digital landscape.

By embracing emotional content as a powerful catalyst, brands are not only adapting to the evolution of digital marketing, but also leading the way to a future where emotional connection becomes the true valuable asset in the digital economy. In this new paradigm, brands are not only selling products, but also weaving emotional stories that linger in the memory of their audience, creating lasting relationships in the vast and ever-changing digital world.

Consumer Psychology in the Digital World: Delving into Emotions

Within the vast spectrum of human emotions, some resonate uniquely in the digital environment. From the thrill of anticipation when opening a package to the instant gratification of a frictionless online experience, every digital interaction can trigger a specific range of emotions. That's why brands can identify these key emotions and use them as building blocks for their emotional content strategies.

- **Neuroscience and Consumer Emotions:**

Neuroscience offers a fascinating window into how the human brain responds to emotional stimuli in the digital world, with research and case studies revealing the secrets behind emotional resonance, from the release of dopamine to the activation of specific brain regions. This science-based approach will enable brands to fine-tune their strategies for deeper and lasting impact.

- **Emerging Trends: Augmented Reality, AI and the Future of Digital Emotions:**

The technological revolution is not standing still, and brands that want to lead the way in building emotional connections must adapt to emerging trends, such as the integration of augmented reality to create immersive experiences, and the growing role of artificial intelligence in personalizing emotional content. These technologies not only add an additional layer of engagement, but also present ethical challenges that brands must carefully address.

- **The Community Manager as Emotion Creator: Practical Strategies:**

We can see how practical strategies for community managers are, highlighting their role as creators of emotions within brands' digital communities. From crisis management to celebrating important milestones, these professionals must be skilled in the art of cultivating positive emotions and efficiently handling delicate emotional situations. We have specific examples of how leading brands have turned their community managers into true emotional architects.

- **Emotional Metrics: Beyond Conventional Numbers:**

Measuring emotional impact is not limited to traditional metrics such as CTR or conversion rate, more advanced emotional metrics, including sentiment analysis in comments and social networks, emotional surveys to assess brand connection, and building custom emotional indexes. These metrics offer a richer and more accurate view of the emotional impact of content strategies.

- **Corporate Social Responsibility (CSR) as a Generator of Emotions:**

In an increasingly conscious digital world, Corporate Social Responsibility (CSR) becomes a vehicle to generate positive emotions, we see how brands can not only communicate their CSR efforts, but also actively engage the audience in initiatives that generate a deep emotional impact. Authenticity and consistency in these actions will be key to building a genuine emotional connection.

- **The Role of the Influencer in Digital Emotionality:**

Influencers have emerged as prominent players in digital storytelling, and their ability to convey authenticity and generate emotion is remarkable, brands can collaborate with influencers strategically to amplify the emotional connection with their audiences. From carefully selecting influencers to creating authentic campaigns, these partnerships can be a powerful driver for building positive emotions.

- **Ethics in Emotional Manipulation: Strategies for Transparency:**

The line between effective persuasion and emotional manipulation is a fine one. And strategies for brands to practice transparency and honesty in their emotional content tactics. These cases where misconduct has damaged brands' reputations, highlighting the importance of building long-term trust through ethical practices.

- **The Path to a Truly Emotional Brand:**

Let's tie all the threads together, highlighting key lessons learned throughout the analysis. being able to affirm that building a truly emotional brand is not just a momentary strategy, but an ongoing commitment to authenticity and human connection. Inspiring brands to embrace the emotional evolution, recognizing that true digital connection is forged not just with products, but with emotional stories that resonate and endure.

What is the opinion of some authors in this regard?

Èlia Guardiola in her article "AWARENESS MARKETING explains what awareness marketing or cause marketing is, and how it can be applied to educate and raise public awareness about different social, environmental and ethical issues. He also gives some examples of successful awareness marketing campaigns, such as Greenpeace, Unicef and Amnesty International.

- ❖ **Bigmentar** In the article "What is humanizing the brand and how to do it?" defines the concept of humanizing the brand as showing the most sensitive and transparent side of the company, and offering personalized and customer-oriented attention. He also gives some tips to show the most human side of the brand, such as communicating with authenticity, showing the work team, telling the brand story, asking for feedback and generating emotions.
- ❖ **Moncloa** In the article "Connecting brands with people in the digital age, with humanized marketing", highlights the importance of humanizing the brand in an increasingly competitive and saturated digital environment, and how humanized marketing can help brands differentiate themselves and create a loyal and engaged community. He also cites some examples of brands that have successfully used humanized marketing, such as Coca-Cola, Dove or Nike.
- ❖ **BSM Digital Marketing** In the article "The importance of emotional branding and brand personality" highlights the role of emotional branding and brand personality in creating an emotional bond with the public, and how these elements can be defined and communicated. He also proposes a brand personality model based on five dimensions: sincerity, emotion, competence, sophistication and robustness.

Navigating the Digital Emotional Future

As we move into the future of digital marketing, building emotional connections becomes more crucial than ever. Evolving trends and technologies challenge us to constantly adapt, but the essence of emotional connection remains unchanged. To guide brands on this journey, it is imperative to remember a few fundamental truths.

First, authenticity is the most valuable currency in the emotional economy. Brands that dare to be genuine, share their stories authentically and show vulnerability earn the trust and loyalty of their audiences. Authenticity is the foundation on which lasting emotional relationships are built.

Second, adaptability becomes an essential virtue. In an ever-changing digital world, brands must be agile, able to adjust their strategies according to emerging trends and changing audience needs. Adaptability ensures that emotional connections evolve with the digital environment.

Third, empathy stands as a vital bridge. Understanding the audience's emotions, putting yourself in their shoes and responding with genuine empathy is what differentiates leading brands. Empathy builds strong emotional bridges, showing the audience that the brand is not only looking to sell products, but also to understand and meet their emotional needs.

In this journey into the digital emotional future, it is also essential to recognize the key role of consumer education. Empowering the audience with information about the brand's values, its social responsibility efforts and the story behind its products contributes to a deeper and more meaningful emotional connection.

The digital emotional future is not just about advanced technology, but about how brands use that technology to build authentic and meaningful experiences. Artificial intelligence and augmented reality become powerful tools, but their implementation must be guided by ethical principles and a desire to enhance emotional connection rather than replace it.

This journey into the digital emotional future is exciting and challenging. Brands that embrace authenticity, adaptability and empathy are best equipped to excel in this evolving landscape. As we move forward, let's remember that emotional connection transcends digital platforms; it is the essence that makes a brand resonate in the heart of its audience. Building strong emotional bridges is not only a smart strategy, but an ongoing commitment to be remembered and loved in the ever-changing digital world.

In the intricate fabric of digital marketing, the emotional connection stands as the backbone that sustains lasting relationships between brands and their audiences. We've explored the anatomy of this connection, from consumer psychology to practical strategies implemented by leading brands. By diving into iconic examples and case studies, we have drawn fundamental lessons that can guide brands in their quest to build emotional bridges in the vast digital landscape.

Digital storytelling has become a story of emotions, where brands not only tell stories, but also become master storytellers of emotional experiences. The evolution of digital marketing urges us to look beyond conventional metrics and understand the emotional impact our strategies can have on consumers' lives.

From brand humanization to emotional personalization, each strategy must be an authentic reflection of the brand's values and identity. The examples of Coca-Cola, Nike and Dove demonstrate that the path to emotional connection involves an ongoing commitment to authenticity, diversity and acceptance.

In social media, building emotional communities has gone from being an option to becoming a necessity. Brands like Airbnb and Starbucks have led the way by creating environments where authenticity and emotional connection flourish. Community managers, now transformed into emotional facilitators, play a crucial role in building and sustaining these digital communities.

Crisis management, as in the Tylenol and Airbnb cases, requires a combination of empathy, transparency and swift action. These difficult moments are crucial tests of emotional connection, and brands that handle these tests with integrity emerge with strengthened confidence.

In the future of digital marketing, technology will continue to be a strategic ally. From augmented reality to artificial intelligence, brands have the opportunity to innovate and personalize emotional experiences more precisely. Ethics will remain an essential guide on this journey, as emotional connection should not be achieved at the expense of privacy or manipulation.

Ultimately, building emotional connections in the digital world is a dynamic and constantly evolving journey. It requires not only astute strategies, but also a deep understanding of human emotions and an ongoing commitment to authenticity. By embracing emotionality as a core principle, brands can not only survive in the changing digital landscape, but also thrive and become unforgettable storytellers in their consumers' emotional story. Emotional connection is not just a strategy; it is the very essence of a brand that transcends digital to become an integral part of the human experience.

CHAPTER IX

The Sales Paradigm in the Digital Age: Navigating the New Sales Horizon

At the intersection of tradition and innovation, the world of sales has undergone an unprecedented metamorphosis in the digital era. The dizzying change in consumer behavior, driven by technological advances and the ubiquity of online connectivity, has forced companies to redefine their commercial strategies. So, we will explore in depth the paradigm of sales in the digital age, unraveling the complexities, highlighting the importance of online presence and offering fundamental strategies to thrive in this new business horizon.

That is why sales is an essential activity for any company that wants to survive and grow in the market. However, the environment in which sales takes place has changed radically in recent years, due to the impact of digitalization and technology. Customers, products, channels, tools and sales strategies have evolved to adapt to the new reality. What does this change imply for companies and salespeople? What are the challenges and opportunities in the digital era? How can technology be leveraged to improve sales and customer satisfaction?

The sales process can be defined as the set of steps that are followed from the time a business opportunity is identified until the sale is closed and the customer becomes loyal. This process may vary according to the type of product, the market, the company and the salesperson, but in general it consists of the following phases: prospecting, contact, presentation, negotiation, closing and post-sale.

In the digital era, this process has undergone a profound transformation, due to several factors:

- **The customer is the protagonist.** Today's customer has more power, information and choice than ever before. Thanks to the Internet and social networks, the customer can access a wealth of information about products, prices, opinions and experiences of other users. The customer can also compare and choose from a wide variety of offers, both local and global. The customer is more demanding, more informed and more critical. For this reason, the salesperson must know the customer, his needs, preferences and motivations. The salesperson must offer a differential value, a customized solution and a positive customer experience. The salesperson must go from being a simple transmitter of information to being an advisor, a consultant and a partner of the customer.

- **The product is more complex**. Today's product is more than a physical good or service. The product is a comprehensive solution that includes aspects such as quality, design, functionality, innovation, sustainability, warranty, support and branding. The product is also more dynamic, as it is constantly updated and improved to adapt to market demands and customer expectations. The product is more customizable, as it can be adapted to the needs and tastes of each customer. Therefore, the salesperson must master the product, its features, its benefits and its competitive advantages. The salesperson must know how to communicate the value of the product, demonstrate how it works, resolve objections and build customer confidence.

- **The channel is more diverse**. The sales channel is the means by which the relationship between the seller and the customer is established. The sales channel can be direct or indirect, physical or virtual, proprietary or external. In the digital era, the sales channel has multiplied and diversified, thanks to the emergence of new digital platforms and tools. The customer can interact with the salesperson through different channels, such as the web, mobile, social networks, email, chat, video, augmented reality, etc. The customer can also combine different channels in their buying process, such as, for example, searching for information on the web, consulting opinions on social networks, contacting the salesperson by phone, visiting the physical store, buying online, receiving the product at home, etc. Therefore, the seller must be present in the channels used by the customer, offer omnichannel service, integrate data from different channels, create a coherent and consistent image across all channels and offer a smooth and satisfactory customer experience.

- The tool is smarter. The sales tool is the resource used by the salesperson to facilitate and improve his work. The sales tool can be material or immaterial, such as, for example, a catalog, a sample, a presentation, a software, a database, etc. In the digital era, the sales tool has become more intelligent, thanks to the advance of technology and digitalization. The salesperson can access a wealth of data and information about the market, the competition, the product, the customer, etc. The salesperson can also use tools such as CRM, email marketing, social selling, SEO, SEM, web analytics, artificial intelligence, big data, blockchain, etc. These tools allow you to optimize your time, automate your tasks, segment your audience, personalize your messages, measure your results and improve your performance.

- The strategy is more flexible. The sales strategy is the plan that defines the objectives, actions, resources and indicators of the commercial activity. The sales strategy must be aligned with the company's overall strategy and marketing plan. In the digital era, the sales strategy must be more flexible, as the environment is more changeable, uncertain and competitive. The salesperson must be attentive to market trends, opportunities and threats. The salesperson must adapt to the needs, expectations and behavior of customers. The salesperson must innovate, experiment and try new ways of selling. The salesperson must continuously evaluate, learn and improve.

- **Sales Process Transformation: Saying Goodbye to the Conventional**

In past decades, sales used to be a field dominated by face-to-face interactions, phone calls and boardroom presentations. However, the digital revolution has broken down geographic and time barriers, giving way to a sales process that unfolds in cyberspace. The virtualization of the buying process has led to the need to rethink and reinvent traditional strategies.

Decision making is now influenced by a diverse range of digital sources. Consumers explore online reviews, participate in virtual communities and compare products before making a purchase decision. In this scenario, deep understanding of the customer journey has become crucial, from awareness to loyalty.

- **The importance of online presence and adaptation to new platforms**

Online presence is the way a company or a vendor displays itself and engages with customers through the Internet and digital platforms. Online presence is critical to sales in the digital age for several reasons:

- Online presence increases visibility and reach. Online presence allows a company or vendor to be found and recognized by potential customers, both locally and globally. Online presence also allows a company or vendor to differentiate and stand out from the competition, creating a unique and attractive brand image.

- **Online presence improves communication and interaction**. Online presence makes it easier for a company or marketer to communicate and interact with current and potential customers quickly, directly and in a personalized way. An online presence also enables a company or marketer to generate and share valuable content that informs, educates, entertains and persuades customers.

- **Online presence builds trust and loyalty**. Online presence helps a company or a vendor to create and maintain a relationship of trust and loyalty with customers by offering quality service, effective customer care, a guarantee of satisfaction and a differential value proposition.

To have an effective online presence, a company or a vendor must adapt to the new platforms that exist in the market, such as:

- **The Web**. The web is the basic platform to have an online presence. A company or a seller must have its own website, which is attractive, functional, updated, secure and adaptable to different devices. The website should contain relevant information about the company, product, service, contact, etc. The website should also be optimized for search engines (SEO), to improve its positioning and organic traffic.

- **Mobile.** Mobile is the platform most used by customers to access the Internet and digital platforms. A company or a vendor must have a mobile presence that is convenient, fast, simple and personalized. A company or a vendor can have a mobile presence through a responsive website, a mobile application (app) or a mobile messaging platform (such as WhatsApp, Telegram, Messenger, etc.). A mobile presence allows a company or vendor to communicate with customers instantly, send notifications, offer promotions, facilitate payment, etc. For example, the transportation company Uber has an app that allows customers to request, pay for and rate the service from their mobile. The fashion company Zara has an app that allows customers to view the catalog, shop online, make in-store reservations, scan products, etc.

- **Social networks**. Social networks are platforms that allow users to create and share content, as well as interact with other users. A company or a vendor must have a social media presence that is active, participatory, consistent and authentic. A company or a marketer can have a social media presence across different platforms, such as Facebook, Instagram, Twitter, LinkedIn, YouTube, TikTok, etc. A social media presence allows a company or marketer to increase visibility, generate traffic, create community, foster engagement, receive feedback, manage reputation, etc.

For example, cosmetics company L'Oréal has a social media presence that allows it to showcase its products, share beauty tips, collaborate with influencers, conduct sweepstakes, etc. Online book seller Amazon has a social media presence that allows it to recommend books, post reviews, create lists, interact with readers, etc.

- **Email**. Email is the platform that allows sending and receiving electronic messages. A company or a marketer must have a professional, personalized, segmented and relevant email presence. A company or a marketer can have an email presence through different tools, such as Mailchimp, HubSpot, Sendinblue, etc. An email presence allows a company or a marketer to communicate with customers in a direct, regular, informative, persuasive, etc. way.

For example, the travel company Booking has an email presence that allows it to send offers, confirmations, reminders, suggestions, etc. Online course seller Udemy has an email presence that allows it to send news, invitations, discounts, certificates, etc.

- **Video**. Video is the platform for creating and transmitting audiovisual content. A company or a marketer must have a video presence that is creative, engaging, educational and emotional. A company or a marketer can have a video presence through different platforms, such as YouTube, Vimeo, Twitch, etc. A video presence allows a company or a marketer to showcase its product, explain how it works, answer questions, share testimonials, tell stories, etc.

For example, technology company Apple has a video presence that allows it to present its products, showcase its features, highlight its benefits, etc. Car vendor Tesla has a video presence that allows it to showcase its cars, explain its technology, share its values, etc.

- **Augmented reality.** Augmented reality is the platform that allows virtual elements to be superimposed on physical reality. A company or a vendor must have a presence in augmented reality that is innovative, interactive, fun and surprising. A company or a marketer can have a presence in augmented reality through different tools, such as Snapchat, Instagram, Facebook, etc. Augmented reality presence allows a company or a vendor to offer an immersive experience, to simulate the use of the product, to personalize the product, to create a viral effect, etc.

For example, the furniture company Ikea has an augmented reality presence that allows customers to see how the furniture would look in their home, change its color, size, position, and so on.

The Ray-Ban eyewear retailer has an augmented reality presence that allows customers to try on the glasses, choose them based on their face shape, share them with friends, etc.

- ### The Importance of Online Presence: Beyond a Stylish Web Site

Online presence is no longer just about having an attractive website. It has become the brand's virtual showcase, where consumers expect to find not only detailed information about products and services, but also an experience that reflects the company's identity and values. Building a strong online presence involves:

1. **Search Engine Optimization (SEO):** Ensure that the brand is easily found in search engines, maximizing online visibility.
2. **Relevant and Engaging Content**: Develop content that educates, entertains and resonates with the audience, establishing the brand as a trusted source.
3. **Active Participation in Social Networks:** Social platforms are not only promotional channels, but also spaces for community building and direct interaction with consumers.
4. **User Experience (UX):** Ensure that navigation through the website is intuitive, efficient and enjoyable, contributing to a positive customer experience.

- **Adaptation to New Platforms: Beyond Resistance to Change**

The constant evolution of digital platforms demands an agile mindset and a willingness to embrace new technologies. Social media, chatbots, artificial intelligence and augmented reality are just some of the elements that are transforming the way we interact and close deals. Here, adaptability becomes an invaluable asset for sales professionals and companies in general.

Social Networks as a Sales Tool: Beyond promotion, social networks have become active sales channels. Platforms such as Instagram and Facebook allow the integration of online stores, facilitating direct purchases from the networks.

Artificial Intelligence (AI) in Personalization: AI offers the ability to analyze massive data and personalize sales interactions, anticipating customer needs and improving the relevance of offers.

Augmented Reality (AR) for Immersive Experiences: In industries such as retail, AR allows customers to visualize products in their environment before purchasing, improving decision making.

- **Strategies for Seizing Technological Opportunities: Beyond Cold Automation**

Technology itself is not a panacea; its effectiveness lies in how it is strategically integrated into sales operations. The following strategies can catalyze leveraging technology opportunities:

Intelligent Automation: Beyond routine automation, intelligent automation uses AI to personalize interactions and improve efficiency at all stages of the sales funnel.

Predictive Analytics: Use predictive analytics tools to anticipate buying behavior, identify opportunities and mitigate risks.

Ongoing Digital Training: Keeping sales teams up to date with the latest digital trends and tools through continuous training programs.

- ## ▪ Strategies to take advantage of the opportunities offered by technology

Technology offers a number of opportunities to improve sales and customer satisfaction in the digital age. However, to take advantage of these opportunities, a company or marketer must follow a number of strategies, such as:

- **Digitization**. Digitization is the strategy of incorporating technology and digitization into all aspects of the business. A company or a salesperson must digitize its processes, products, channels, tools and sales strategies. Digitization allows a company or a vendor to be more efficient, more agile, more competitive and more innovative. For example, the food delivery company Glovo has digitized its sales process, allowing customers to order, pay and receive their order from their cell phones. Appliance retailer MediaMarkt has digitized its product, offering smart products that connect to the Internet and are controlled from the cell phone.

- **Personalization**. Personalization is the strategy of tailoring the product, service, message and experience to the customer, taking into account his characteristics, needs, preferences and behavior. A company or a salesperson must personalize its offer, its communication, its service and its relationship with the customer. Personalization allows a company or a salesperson to increase customer satisfaction, loyalty, recommendation and value. For example, sportswear company Nike has personalized its offer, allowing customers to design their own sneakers, choosing the color, model, name, etc. Online music retailer Spotify has personalized its communication, sending customers playlists, suggestions, statistics, etc. based on their tastes and music habits.

- **Automation**. Automation is the strategy of using technology and artificial intelligence to perform repetitive, routine or complex tasks that previously required human intervention. A company or a salesperson must automate its tasks, processes, actions and sales decisions. Automation allows a company or a salesperson to save time, money, resources and errors. For example, shipping company DHL has automated its tasks, using robots, drones and autonomous vehicles to transport and deliver packages. Online insurance seller Coverfy has automated its processes, using a chatbot that advises, contracts and manages customers' insurance.

- Integration. Integration is the strategy of connecting and coordinating the different elements involved in the sales activity, such as products, channels, tools, data, teams, etc. A company or a salesperson must integrate its elements, creating a network of collaboration, information and value. Integration enables a company or a vendor to improve its quality, coherence, consistency and competitiveness. For example, fashion company H&M has integrated its elements, creating a platform that connects its physical stores, its online store, its app, its loyalty program, its stock, its suppliers, etc. Online software vendor Microsoft has integrated its elements, creating a suite that integrates its products, such as Word, Excel, PowerPoint, Outlook, Teams, etc.

- Innovation. Innovation is the strategy of creating and offering something new, different and better, which brings value to the customer and the market. A company or a vendor must innovate in its products, services, channels, tools and sales strategies. Innovation allows a company or a vendor to differentiate, stand out, adapt and anticipate. For example, the entertainment company Netflix has innovated in its service, offering a streaming service of movies and series, with a wide, varied and original catalog, with an affordable price and customer customization. Online book seller Bookmate has innovated its channel, offering a social reading channel, allowing customers to read, share, comment and discover books, with other readers and authors.

▪ Redefining the Role of the Sales Professional in the Digital Age: Beyond the Transaction

In this new paradigm, the role of the sales professional is redefined as a strategic advisor and problem solver. The ability to understand customer needs, interpret digital data and build authentic relationships becomes as crucial as closing a transaction. The sale is no longer a one-time event, but an integral part of the customer journey.

▪ Case Study: Companies That Have Successfully Embraced Digital Transformation

To illustrate the practical application of these strategies, we will examine cases of companies that have led the digital transformation in their industries. From the effective adoption of social networks to the implementation of artificial intelligence tools, these companies have demonstrated that digital innovation is not just a luxury, but a necessity for survival and sustainable growth.

Amazon: The Continuing Disruption in E-Commerce

1. Amazon has used technology to optimize the customer experience from search to delivery.
2. Established personalization and recommendation strategies that have led to a significant increase in conversions.

Salesforce: Leading in Automation and Artificial Intelligence

1. Salesforce's focus on intelligent automation and AI integration into its CRM platform.
2. How these tools have improved the sales team's efficiency

Tesla: Reinventing the Automotive Shopping Experience

1. Tesla's unique strategy of selling directly to the consumer, eliminating middlemen.
2. It uses technology, such as online purchasing mode and software updates, this has been Tesla's core value proposition.

- **Challenges and Ethical Considerations in the Digital Age of Sales: Beyond Technology Euphoria**

As we dive into this exciting chapter of sales, we must also recognize and address ethical challenges. Massive data collection, customer privacy and the risk of over-reliance on technology are concerns that should not be overlooked. Ethics in digital sales is not only a responsibility, but also an opportunity to build a solid reputation and earn long-term customer trust.

- **Navigating Towards a Sustainable and Successful Commercial Future**

In the digital age of sales, adaptability and effective technology integration are key to success. The transformation of the sales process, the importance of a strategic online presence and the implementation of emerging technologies are not only imperative, but also exciting opportunities to innovate and lead in the marketplace.

Sales professionals must not only be experts in products or services, but also in technology and human understanding. Emotional connection, albeit facilitated by digital platforms, remains at the core of successful sales. Shoppers are looking not only for quality products, but also for meaningful experiences and authentic relationships with brands.

The digital age of sales represents not only a paradigm shift, but an invitation to a new era of creativity, adaptability and collaboration. By seizing technological opportunities, addressing ethical challenges and prioritizing emotional connection, companies can not only survive in this new horizon, but also thrive and lead in the constant redefinition of the world of sales. In this journey into the commercial future, technology is the compass, but authenticity and empathy remain the rudder that guides toward a destination of sustainable success.

The Evolution of the Sales Professional in the Digital Age: Beyond Closing Transactions

The sales professional has undergone a metamorphosis in the digital era. It is no longer just about closing transactions, but about building long-term relationships. Adaptability and a willingness to continually learn become essential. Today's successful salespeople must be tech-savvy, understand consumer psychology and be adept at interpreting data.

Digital Skills Development: The ability to use digital tools, understand analytics and adapt to new platforms becomes a critical component of the modern sales professional's skill set.

Customer Orientation: In an environment where competition is a click away, customer-centric focus becomes a key differentiator. Understanding customer needs and expectations, and anticipating them, becomes critical.

Continuous Learning: The speed at which technology evolves drives the need for continuous learning. Sales professionals must be willing to acquire new skills and stay current on the latest trends and tools.

- **Strategies for Leveraging Online Presence: Beyond Conventional Marketing**

Online presence goes beyond having a functional website. It involves creating a digital experience that not only attracts customers, but also retains them and turns them into brand advocates.

Personalized Content: Creating relevant and personalized content becomes a powerful tool to attract the right audience. Using data analytics to understand customer interests allows you to deliver content that resonates with them.

Active Social Media Engagement: Go beyond posting content and actively participate in social media conversations. Authentic interactions build a deeper connection with the audience.

Dynamic SEO Strategies: Keeping up to date with SEO best practices and adapting strategies according to changing search engine trends and algorithms.

- **Adaptation to New Platforms: Beyond Presence Alone**

Presence on new platforms involves more than simply signing up for them. It requires a deep understanding of how to use these platforms to build relationships and close sales.

Strategic Use of Social Networks: Each social network has its own dynamics. Sales professionals must understand the distinctive characteristics of each platform and adapt their strategies accordingly.

Chatbots and Virtual Assistants: Effective implementation of chatbots and virtual assistants not only improves efficiency, but also provides customers with instant and personalized responses.

Immersive Experiences: In sectors such as fashion and tourism, virtual and augmented reality can be used to offer customers immersive experiences, allowing them to interact with products or destinations before making a purchase.

Ethical Challenges and Privacy Considerations: Beyond Technological Benefits

Massive data collection and the implementation of advanced technologies pose significant ethical challenges. Customer privacy must be a priority, and companies must be transparent about how they use data.

Data Collection Ethics: Companies should establish clear policies on how customer data is collected, stored and used. Transparency and obtaining consent become essential practices.

Information Security: Ensuring the security of customer information is becoming critical. Companies must invest in robust security measures to protect confidential information.

Balance between Personalization and Privacy: Personalization is key in the digital age, but it must be balanced with respect for privacy. Strategies must avoid intrusion and the perception of constant surveillance.

▪ The Future of Sales: Beyond Technological Innovation

The future of sales is intrinsically linked to the ability of companies and sales professionals to constantly innovate. Beyond the implementation of emerging technologies, innovation involves the ability to anticipate trends and anticipate market needs.

Emerging Trends: Exploring trends that are on the horizon, such as advanced artificial intelligence, enhanced virtual reality and even deeper integration of predictive analytics.

Interdisciplinary Collaboration: Collaboration between sales, marketing and technology teams becomes essential. The synergy between these disciplines allows for more effective implementation of innovative strategies.

Focus on Customer Experience: The future of sales will be centered on the customer experience. From the first interaction to post-sales support, every touch point must contribute to a positive and memorable experience.

▪ The Role of the Business Leader: Beyond Conventional Supervision

In the digital age, business leadership requires a unique combination of strategic vision, technology skills and a focused approach to talent development.

Transformational Leadership: Leaders must adopt a transformational approach, driving innovation and fostering a culture that embraces change.

Digital Talent Development: Investing in the development of digital skills of the team becomes crucial. Ongoing training and mentoring programs can be effective tools.

Long-Term Strategic Vision: Business leaders must look beyond immediate profits and take a long-term strategic view that anticipates future market needs.

Pathway to Excellence in the Digital Sales Era

The digital age of sales represents an exciting journey to business excellence, but it also presents significant challenges. The ability to adapt to new technologies, build authentic relationships and address ethical considerations become the foundation on which success is built.

Sales professionals, business leaders and companies in general must embrace the mindset of continuous adaptability and constant innovation. In this ever-changing business horizon, the ability to anticipate, adapt and lead will be the key to not only survive, but also excel and thrive in the new era of digital sales.

- ## Recommendations to Succeed in the Digital Age of Sales: Practical Strategies
  - To achieve success in the digital age of sales, it is essential to implement practical, results-oriented strategies. Here are some key recommendations:

Adopt a Customer-Centric Mentality:

Understand the customer's changing needs and desires.

Personalize interactions and offers to build long-term relationships.

Invest in Continuing Education:

- Develop digital skills of the team through continuous training programs.
- Keeping up to date with the latest trends and technologies.

Maximize Online Presence:

- Go beyond having a website and create an immersive digital experience.
- Use effective SEO strategies to improve online visibility.

Exploiting Social Networking Opportunities:

- Actively participate in conversations in social networks.
- Use platforms as direct sales and community building tools.

Integrating Emerging Technologies with Prudence:

- Evaluate and select technologies that align with business goals.
- Ensure ethics in the collection and use of data.

Prioritize Ethics and Privacy:

- Establish clear policies on the collection and use of customer data.

- Maintain customer privacy as a priority in all interactions.

Cultivate a Culture of Innovation:

- Encourage cross-functional collaboration between sales, marketing and technology teams.
- Stimulate an innovation mindset that constantly seeks new opportunities and solutions.

▪ Achieving Success in the Digital Sales Revolution

The digital age of sales is not simply a change in the way we transact; it is a revolution that fundamentally redefines the relationship between brands and consumers. In this journey, we have explored how the transformation of the sales process, the importance of a strategic online presence and the implementation of emerging technologies form the essence of the commercial evolution.

- ✓ The ability to adapt to new platforms, build authentic relationships and address ethical challenges has been highlighted as imperative for continued success. Sales professionals, business leaders and companies must embrace this constant change and cultivate a continuous learning mindset.
- ✓ As we look to the future, excellence in the digital age of sales is not just about closing transactions, but building meaningful experiences that resonate with customers. Constant innovation, adaptability and prioritizing human connection will continue to be the pillars of sustainable success.

Let's remember that every digital interaction is an opportunity to build an emotional bridge to the customer. By successfully navigating this digital sales revolution, we build not just transactions, but lasting, meaningful relationships that are the foundation for a prosperous business future.

Recommendations

To cope with the sales paradigm in the digital era, a company or a salesperson should consider the following recommendations:

- **Keeping up with the times.** The digital era is characterized by constant change, uncertainty and competition. For this reason, a company or a salesperson must keep abreast of market trends, opportunities and threats, as well as new developments, tools and digital platforms. A company or a salesperson must be trained, informed and continuously updated, in order not to be left behind and to offer a differential value to the customer.

- **Listen to the customer**. The customer is the center of the commercial activity, the one who has the power, the information and the options. That is why a company or a salesperson must listen to the customer, his needs, his preferences and his opinions. A company or a salesperson must collect and analyze customer data and feedback, to know the customer better, to offer a customized solution and to improve customer satisfaction.

- Provide value. Value is what makes a customer choose one offer over another, what satisfies him, what makes him loyal. Therefore, a company or a salesperson must provide value to the customer by offering a quality product or service that solves their problem, meets their needs, and exceeds their expectations. A company or a salesperson must communicate the value of its offer, demonstrating how it works, resolving objections and generating confidence in the customer.

- Be creative. Creativity is the ability to create and offer something new, different and better that brings value to the customer and the market. Therefore, a company or a salesperson must be creative, innovating in their products, services, channels, tools and sales strategies. A company or a salesperson must surprise, excite, amuse and convince the customer with a unique and attractive value proposition.

- Being human. Humanity is the quality of being sensitive, empathetic, honest and ethical, which generates an emotional connection with the customer. Therefore, a company or a salesperson must be human, treating the customer with respect, closeness, kindness and professionalism. A company or a salesperson must create and maintain a relationship of trust and loyalty with the customer, offering quality service, effective customer service, a guarantee of satisfaction and a differential value proposition.

Sales is an essential activity for any company that wants to survive and grow in the market. However, sales is not a static activity; it evolves over time, adapting to changes in the environment, the market and the customer. In the digital era, sales has undergone a profound transformation, involving a number of challenges and opportunities for companies and salespeople. To meet these challenges and take advantage of these opportunities, companies and salespeople must incorporate technology and digitization into all aspects of their commercial activity, offering differential value to the customer, through an effective online presence, offer personalization, task automation, integration of elements and constant innovation. Thus, companies and vendors will be able to improve their sales and customer satisfaction, creating a competitive advantage and a unique and attractive value proposition.

Sales in the digital age is a paradigm that requires constant adaptation, updating and creativity, but also offers an opportunity for growth, learning and continuous improvement. Sales in the digital era is a challenge, but also an opportunity. An opportunity to create and offer solutions that bring value to the customer and the market, that generate an emotional connection with the customer and that contribute to a more sustainable, more inclusive and more human future. Sales in the digital age is an opportunity to make the world a better place.

The sales paradigm in the digital era is a complex, dynamic and challenging phenomenon, which implies a profound transformation of the commercial activity. This transformation affects all the elements involved in the sales process, such as the customer, the product, the channel, the tool and the strategy. This transformation also offers a number of opportunities to improve sales and customer satisfaction, such as visibility, communication, trust, personalization, automation, integration and innovation.

However, to take advantage of these opportunities, a company or a salesperson must adapt to the new reality, incorporating technology and digitalization in all aspects of its commercial activity. A company or a salesperson must know the customer well, their needs, preferences and motivations. A company or a salesperson must master the product, its characteristics, its benefits and its competitive advantages. A company or a salesperson must be present in the channels used by the customer, offer an omnichannel service, integrate data from different channels and offer a smooth and satisfactory customer experience. A company or a salesperson must use tools that facilitate and improve their work, optimize their time, automate their tasks, segment their audience, personalize their messages, measure their results and improve their performance. A company or a salesperson must follow a flexible strategy that adapts to the needs, expectations and behavior of customers, that innovates, experiments and tries new ways of selling, that evaluates, learns and improves continuously.

CHAPTER X

The New Sales Technique "Strategic FUSION": Connecting Face-to-Face and Virtual for Success

In a world where face-to-face and virtual sales coexist, it is essential to design a technique that capitalizes on the strengths of both modalities. The "Strategic FUSION" technique focuses on the harmonious integration of face-to-face and virtual strategies, providing a complete experience adapted to the current characteristics of salespeople. From greeting to closing, this technique seeks to optimize each interaction.

It is important to adapt to the current context, where virtual sales have become more relevant due to the pandemic and the mobility restrictions that were experienced, that is why we will analyze some of the known sales techniques have had to vary in form but not in substance, having to combine the techniques of face-to-face and virtual sales, taking advantage of the best of each, highlighting the following aspects

- Use videoconferencing tools to create a more personal connection with the customer and show the product or service in a dynamic and visual way.
- Apply inbound marketing to engage and educate prospects with content that is valuable and relevant to their needs and problems.
- Implement a CRM to manage and automate the sales process, from the first contact to closing and loyalty.
- Segment and personalize messages and offers according to each customer's profile, behavior and level of interest.
- Use artificial intelligence and data analytics to optimize sales strategies and improve sales team performance.

As we can see, any change requires greater adaptability, so some of the benefits of hybrid sales are:

- Extend the reach and accessibility of customers, without being limited by distance or time.
- Reduce costs and resources associated with travel and face-to-face visits.
- Increase the flexibility and adaptability of salespeople, who can choose the most appropriate channel for each situation and customer.
- Improve the experience and satisfaction of customers, who can receive faster, more convenient and personalized service.

It is important to integrate sales techniques, as each one provides key elements for commercial success. However, it is not a matter of applying them in isolation or mechanically, but of adapting them to the context, the product or service, and the customer. Below, I will briefly summarize what each of the most commonly used techniques consists of and how you could use them in the new hybrid model:

SPIN: is based on asking the customer four types of questions: situation, problem, involvement and need. The objective is to identify their needs, generate urgency and offer a solution. You could use this technique to qualify the customer and present your value proposition.

Collaborative selling: is based on establishing a relationship of trust and cooperation with the customer, involving them in the sales process and seeking their feedback. The goal is to create a joint solution that benefits both parties. You could use this technique to generate commitment and loyalty with the customer.

Use of positive testimonials: this is based on showing the customer success stories and opinions of other customers satisfied with the product or service. The objective is to generate credibility and trust, and reduce objections. You could use this technique to reinforce your argumentation and demonstrate the value of your offer.

SNAP: is based on four principles: simple, invaluable, aligned and prioritized. The objective is to facilitate the customer's decision making by offering them a solution that is simple, valuable, aligned with their objectives and prioritized for their business. You could use this technique to differentiate yourself from the competition and accelerate closing.

Consultative selling: is based on acting as a consultant or advisor to the customer, providing information, knowledge and solutions to their problems. The goal is to create a relationship of trust and credibility, and to position yourself as an expert in the industry. You could use this technique to educate and guide the customer through the buying process.

Challenger or challenging salesperson: is based on challenging the customer with innovative and disruptive ideas that make them question their current situation and see new opportunities. The objective is to generate curiosity and interest, and show the customer how he can improve his situation with the product or service. You could use this technique to capture the customer's attention and interest, and differentiate yourself from the competition.

Sandler: based on inverting the traditional sales process, making the customer sell his need to the salesperson, and not the other way around. The objective is to avoid pressure and manipulation, and make the customer convince himself that he needs the product or service. You could use this technique to avoid objections and rejection, and build trust and respect with the customer.

Storytelling: it is based on telling a story that connects with the customer, makes him feel emotions and conveys a message. The objective is to capture the customer's attention and interest, and to persuade them in a subtle and attractive way. You could use this technique to present your product or service, to tell success stories, or to create a personal connection with the customer.

AICDC: is based on following five steps: attention, interest, conviction, desire and closing. The objective is to guide the customer through the sales process, from capturing their attention to closing the deal. You could use this technique as a general structure for your sales process, adapting it to each case and customer.

FAB: is based on highlighting the features, advantages and benefits of the product or service. The objective is to show the customer how the product or service can satisfy their needs and solve their problems. You could use this technique to present your offer to the customer, focusing on the benefits it brings.

As you can see, there are many sales techniques that you can use, but the most important thing is that you adapt them to your reality and that of your customers. It is for this reason that after having carried out a rigorous investigation, it has been possible to elaborate a new sales technique in which the Presential and Virtual are merged into one and it is detailed below:

I. FUSION" Salutation: Creating a Powerful Initial Connection

Classroom and Virtual:

- Initiate the interaction with a friendly and professional greeting, adapted to the face-to-face or virtual environment.
  Face-to-face example: Shake hands with a warm smile.
  Virtual Example: Use a friendly greeting through the camera with a personalized introduction.

Multichannel Presentation:

- Briefly introduce yourself and mention the possibility of interaction both in person and virtually.

Example, "It's a pleasure to meet you in person, and I'm also excited to connect virtually if we ever need to delve into more specific details."

II. Exploration "FUSION": Adapting to the Client's Needs

Classroom and Virtual:

- Use situational questions in both face-to-face and virtual environments to explore client needs.

Presential Example: "Tell me, how has your experience been at this event so far?"

Virtual Example: "In the virtual environment, unique challenges often arise. Is there something specific you are looking to improve in your digital strategy?"

Multichannel Platform:

- Mention the availability on multiple platforms for ongoing consultation and discussion.

Example: "In addition to our face-to-face meetings, I am always available to discuss any questions or details via video call or email."

III. FUSION" Collaboration: Co-Creating Impactful Solutions

Classroom and Virtual:

- Invite the client to actively participate in the creation of solutions both in face-to-face and virtual meetings.

Presential Example: "Let's collaborate on this board to outline together how we can address your needs."

Virtual Example: "On our shared screen, we can work together to customize a solution that perfectly fits your situation."

Hybrid Demonstration:

- Conduct demonstrations that leverage the strengths of face-to-face and virtual interaction.

Example: "In the room, I can physically show you how our product works, and then, on the screen, we will detail its additional benefits and virtual features."

IV. Testimonials "FUSION": Building Trust from Both Worlds

Classroom and Virtual:

- Incorporate testimonials from both face-to-face and virtual experiences to support the effectiveness of the solution.

In-person example: "We have received outstanding feedback from clients who have experienced significant results from events like this."

Virtual Example: "On our online platform, customer testimonials highlight how we have transformed their operations virtually."

Integrated Stories:

- Build stories that connect face-to-face experiences with virtual successes and vice versa.

Example: "Let me share how an initial face-to-face meeting led to a successful virtual collaboration that resulted in significant growth for our client."

V. SNAP Sale "FUSION": Creating Urgency and Value in Both Worlds

Classroom and Virtual:

- Use the SNAP technique to highlight the Situation, Need, Alternative and Perceived Benefit in both face-to-face and virtual contexts.

Example: "Given the current market situation, it is essential to consider an alternative such as ours that can offer immediate benefits in both physical and digital environments."

VI. FUSION" Consultative Selling: Guiding with Depth in Both Environments

Complete Understanding:

- Deepen understanding of both the client's face-to-face and virtual objectives.

Example: "To offer the best solution, I need to understand in detail your business goals in this new paradigm, whether in physical events or digital interactions."

Multichannel Personalized Advice:

- Offer personalized recommendations based on the information collected, adapting them to both environments.

Example: "Based on your on-site and virtual situation, I suggest this configuration that has proven to be highly effective for similar companies."

VII. Challenger "FUSION": Challenging Perspectives in Both Worlds

Classroom and Virtual:

- To pose challenging questions that stimulate reflection in both face-to-face and virtual environments.

Presential Example: "How could you integrate our solution into your events to maximize your impact?"

Virtual Example: "Let's talk about how our technology could challenge your current digital approach to achieve even more remarkable results."

VIII. Venta Sandler "FUSION": Managing Conversation in Different Spaces

Presential and Virtual Agreement:

- Establish step-by-step agreements in both face-to-face and virtual meetings.

Example, "Would you agree to explore how we can move forward together in both our in-person meetings and our virtual sessions?"

Handling Objections in Both Worlds:

- Anticipate and handle objections in both face-to-face and virtual environments.

Example, "I understand your concerns about virtual integration; let me share how we have successfully addressed this challenge with other clients, both in physical and digital events."

IX. Storytelling Sales Technique "FUSION": Creating Narratives That Resonate Across Channels

Classroom and Virtual:

- Build stories that transcend the customer's face-to-face and virtual experiences.

Example: "Let me tell you how an initial connection at a face-to-face event led to a successful collaboration that blossomed in the virtual world."

Integrated Emotion:

- Incorporate emotional elements that resonate in both worlds, face-to-face and virtual.

Example: "Imagine the excitement you will feel when you see the tangible impact of our solution, either in your office or through a screen."

X. AICDC "FUSION" Model: A Structured Guide to Integral Success

Comprehensive Care:

- Capture the customer's attention with an approach that adapts to both face-to-face and virtual environments.

Example: "Before I finish, I want to highlight how our solution can transform your experience, whether it's physical events or virtual meetings."

Continuous Interest:

- Maintain customer interest through targeted data and benefits, addressing their needs in both worlds.

Example: "Based on your specific needs, I see great potential to improve your results in your face-to-face and virtual events."

Integrated locking:

- Use closing techniques adapted to both face-to-face and virtual environments.

Example: "Given the obvious advantages offered by our solution, would you like to take the next step to implement it in both your physical events and your digital strategies?"

XI. FUSION" Technique: Incorporation of Innovative Elements

Augmented and Virtual Reality:

- Use augmented and virtual reality technologies to enhance the customer experience, either in face-to-face events or virtual sessions.

Example: "Let's experience how our solution integrates into your physical space using augmented reality."

Real-Time Collaboration Tools:

- Implement real-time collaboration tools that facilitate active participation in both face-to-face and virtual meetings.

Example: "During our virtual meeting, we will use this tool to sketch together ideas and customize the solution according to your needs."

The "Strategic FUSION" technique embraces the hybrid reality of modern sales, leveraging the best of the face-to-face and virtual worlds. By adapting to the characteristics of new salespeople and the dynamics of the current era, this technique seeks not only to close transactions, but to build authentic connections that transcend physical and digital barriers. Let every interaction under "Strategic FUSION" be a step towards comprehensive success in 21st century sales. Let the connection be complete and lasting!

PRACTICAL EXAMPLE OF THE NEW SALES TECHNIQUE

XII. Case Study "FUSION": Integrating the Best of Both Worlds

Context:

A consulting firm implements the "Strategic FUSION" technique in its sales approach to adapt to the hybrid reality of the market.

Stages of the Technique:

Greeting "FUSION":

During in-person events, representatives greet attendees in the traditional way, but also promote virtual connections for those who prefer to interact digitally.

Exploration "FUSION":

A specific application is developed to collect data and customer needs in both physical events and digital interactions.

Collaboration "FUSION":

During face-to-face meetings, whiteboards and interactive materials are used. In virtual sessions, screens are shared and active participation is encouraged through online collaboration tools.

Testimonials "FUSION":

A library of testimonials is created that address both in-person and virtual customer experiences, supporting the versatility of the solution.

SNAP "FUSION" sale:

Exclusive offers are designed for physical and digital events, creating a sense of urgency and value in both the real and virtual worlds.

Consultative Sale "FUSION":

Consultants use data analysis of both face-to-face and virtual interactions to provide customized recommendations tailored to each environment.

Challenger "FUSION":

Strategic challenges are raised during physical and digital demonstrations, instigating deep thinking about how the solution can transform your operations.

Venta Sandler "FUSION":

Agreements and commitments are established both in face-to-face meetings and in virtual sessions, ensuring a smooth progression in both contexts.

Storytelling "FUSION":

Captivating narratives are built around experiences that merge face-to-face and digital events, highlighting cases where collaboration began in one environment and expanded to the other.

AICDC "FUSION" Model:

The AICDC structure is consistently applied in face-to-face and virtual presentations to guide clients from attention to closing.

FUSION" technique:

Innovative tools are implemented, such as virtual reality for demonstrations and real-time collaboration platforms, creating unique experiences adapted to each context.

Result:

The company experiences a significant increase in conversions and customer satisfaction. The ability to adapt fluidly to customer preferences and changing market dynamics positions the company as a sales leader in both the face-to-face and virtual worlds.

These success stories demonstrate the versatility and effectiveness of the "Strategic FUSION" technique by integrating the best of both worlds, creating holistic sales experiences tailored to today's consumer and business realities.

XIII. Final Analysis and Recommendations for Vendors in the "FUSION" Era

Essential Skills for Sellers in the "FUSION" Era:

Technological Adaptability:

The ability to use digital tools and virtual platforms is crucial for effective interaction in face-to-face and virtual environments.

Collaboration Skills:

The ability to work collaboratively, either on a physical whiteboard during a face-to-face meeting or through online collaboration tools in virtual sessions.

Compelling Narrative:

The ability to build stories that connect face-to-face and virtual experiences, generating a lasting emotional impact on customers.

Integral Product Knowledge:

A thorough understanding of how the solution can adapt and benefit both in-person events and digital strategies is essential to effective selling.

Urgency and Courage Management:

Develop skills to create a sense of urgency and value in both face-to-face and virtual situations, using the SNAP technique strategically.

Challenging Thinking:

The ability to challenge perspectives, instigating critical reflection on how the solution can transform operations in both the real and digital worlds.

Management of Virtual Sales Tools:

Master virtual sales tools, including collaborative platforms, augmented reality and other emerging technologies.

Adaptability in Sales Closing:

Be able to adapt closing techniques to face-to-face and virtual environments, ensuring an effective conclusion in both modalities.

Final Recommendations for "FUSION" Vendors:

Continuous Research:

Keep abreast of the latest technology and sales trends to constantly adapt to a changing environment.

Virtual Skills Development:

Invest time in honing the skills necessary for effective selling in virtual environments, including platform management and screen-based communication.

Interdepartmental Collaboration:

Collaborate closely with marketing and technology teams to ensure seamless integration between face-to-face and virtual strategies.

Continuous Training:

Participate in training programs that address the skills needed for the "FUSION" era, including adaptation to face-to-face and virtual sales dynamics.

Epic Conclusion for the "FUSION" Era:

In this era of mergers, where the physical and the virtual converge in a harmonious dance, salespeople find themselves in an exciting and challenging scenario. The "Strategic FUSION" technique represents not only an intelligent adaptation to changes in the world of sales, but also a celebration of the human capacity to evolve and thrive in changing environments.

For bold and visionary salespeople who embrace this "FUSION" philosophy, the rewards are monumental. It's not just about closing transactions, but building lasting relationships that transcend physical and digital limitations. It is the art of merging the tangible with the intangible, creating experiences that resonate in the heart and on the screen.

In the "FUSION" era, marketers are architects of connections, weavers of narratives that straddle the palpable and the virtual. Every interaction is an opportunity to build bridges that connect face-to-face and digital experiences, shaping a future where sales are not simply transactions, but holistic experiences.

May every marketer become a master of "FUSION", creating symphonies that resonate on every screen and corner of the physical world. In this exciting era, where the boundaries between the real and the virtual are blurring, "FUSION" salespeople are the architects of a tomorrow that is more connected, more human and more successful than ever before. May "FUSION" inspire and elevate every salesperson to new heights of achievement and impactful connections!

In the vibrant symphony of the "FUSION" era, marketers are the protagonists of an ever-evolving story. Every interaction, whether in the palpable world of face-to-face events or in the limitless realm of the digital sphere, is an opportunity to write an extraordinary chapter in the book of human connections.

The ability to embrace "Strategic FUSION" lies not only in the mastery of digital tools or a deep understanding of traditional selling; it lies in the ability to transcend barriers and adapt to the constant dance between the tangible and the intangible. It is the art of weaving experiences that know no geographical boundaries or screen limitations.

On this exciting journey, each "FUSION" salesperson becomes a storyteller of unforgettable experiences. He is an architect of bridges that connect seemingly disparate worlds, reminding us that, ultimately, sales is a sublime expression of human connection.

So, dear "FUSION" marketers, let's move forward with courage and creativity. Let us continue to build bridges that bring hearts together, whether in the warmth of a handshake or the effervescence of a virtual conversation. May every customer become a fellow traveler on this sales odyssey, and may each connection transcend physical and digital limitations.

In the "FUSION" era, where face-to-face and virtual converge, selling is more than a transaction; it is a symphony in which every salesperson is a conductor, every customer is a protagonist and every connection is a masterpiece.

May the "FUSION OF SALES TECHNIQUES" inspire our journey, raise our expectations and propel us into a future where sales is not just a business function, but a sublime expression of humanity in its truest form. May "SALES" continue to resonate in every interaction and may every salesperson write a legendary chapter in the chronicle of this exciting and innovative era!

What do we expect in the next 5 years?

This response involves considering current trends, changes in consumer behavior and technological developments. Although it is not possible to provide future data, it is possible to suggest some emerging trends that could influence sales techniques in the near future:

Data Driven Personalization:

Data analytics will become even more crucial to understanding customers on an individual level. Sales techniques will focus on personalizing messages and offers based on demographics, buying behaviors and preferences.

Artificial Intelligence (AI) in Sales:

The integration of artificial intelligence in sales processes will expand. Advanced chatbots, predictive analytics and automation of repetitive tasks will enable sales teams to focus on more strategic activities.

Data-Centric Customer Experience (CX):

Sales techniques will become more closely aligned with improving the customer experience. Real-time feedback and customer satisfaction analysis will be critical to adjust sales strategies.

Social Selling and Professional Networking:

The use of social media and professional platforms for lead generation and relationship building will continue to be a growing trend. The ability to connect with potential customers through social channels will be essential.

Educational Content and Storytelling:

Sales techniques will focus on providing educational content that solves customer problems. Storytelling will continue to be a powerful tool to connect emotionally with customers.

Hybrid Sales (Face-to-Face and Virtual):

The pandemic has accelerated the adoption of virtual sales. Sales techniques will adapt to hybrid models that leverage the best of face-to-face and virtual interactions to reach a wider audience.

Technology-Enhanced Consultative Selling:

Consultative selling will be strengthened with technological tools that enable salespeople to better understand customer needs and offer customized solutions.

Emphasis on Sustainability and Ethics:

Consumers are increasingly concerned about sustainability and business ethics. Effective sales techniques will incorporate messages and business practices aligned with sustainable and ethical values.

Virtual Reality (VR) and Augmented Reality (AR):

For products or services that require visual demonstration, VR and AR will be powerful tools. Sales techniques could leverage these technologies to deliver immersive experiences.

Automation of Complex Sales Processes:

In B2B sales, especially in industries with complex purchasing processes, automation of certain steps of the sales process will be a trend, enabling greater efficiency.

In the B2C arena, sales techniques will be even more focused on creating personalized and engaging shopping experiences. Considering the direct and emotional nature of B2C transactions, strategies will focus on capturing attention, building trust and providing solutions tailored to individual consumer needs.

It is essential to continually adapt to emerging trends and leverage technology to improve sales strategies. In addition, the ability to maintain a customer-centric approach will be key to success in the coming years.

Real Time Interactivity:

Real-time interactivity, through features such as virtual demos, live Q&A sessions and videoconferencing, will become an essential technique for building strong customer relationships and closing sales, so we will need to consider the following aspects.

Gamification in Sales:

Gamification, applying gaming elements to the sales process, will be used to motivate sales teams, improve customer engagement and create more engaging experiences.

Strategic Use of E-Commerce Platforms:

E-commerce platforms will evolve, and sales techniques will adapt to take full advantage of these platforms. The integration of direct purchasing tools and frictionless shopping experiences will be crucial.

Integrated Multichannel Approach:

Sales techniques will focus on an integrated multichannel approach, where message consistency and customer experience will be maintained across multiple channels, whether physical or virtual.

Machine Learning for Behavior Prediction:

Machine learning and advanced analytics will be used to predict customer behavior, enabling sales teams to anticipate needs, personalize offers and improve conversion rates.

Collaboration between Sales and Marketing Teams:

Alignment and close collaboration between sales and marketing teams will intensify. Coordinated strategies will ensure a smooth transition from lead generation to sales closure.

Social Selling 2.0:

Social selling will evolve into a second phase where authenticity, genuine engagement and building strong relationships in digital environments will stand out as effective strategies.

Cybersecurity in Commercial Transactions:

Given the growing importance of online security, sales techniques will be adapted to address customer security concerns by implementing robust measures to ensure secure transactions.

Real Time Sentiment Analysis:

Tools that analyze customer sentiment in real time will be critical. This will allow marketers to adjust their approach according to the customer's emotional responses during interactions.

Development of Socioemotional Skills:

As automation becomes more prominent, social-emotional skills, such as empathy, effective communication and emotional intelligence, will be more highly valued in sales professionals to build meaningful connections.

In the coming years, effective sales techniques will be intrinsically linked to adaptability, technological innovation and a deep understanding of customer needs. Strategies that focus on personalization, emerging technology and emotional connection will continue to lead the way. The ability to embrace change and continually learn will be essential for sales professionals looking to excel in a dynamic and constantly evolving business environment.

CHAPTER XI

Neuro Marketing and Brainketing: A Brain Journey in the Post-Pandemic Digital Age

In the dynamic universe of marketing, Neuro Marketing and its evolution, embodied in the broader concept of Brainketing, have emerged as crucial disciplines for understanding and shaping consumer behavior. The pandemic has been a catalyst for profound changes in society and, consequently, in marketing strategies. In this article, we will explore how Neuro Marketing and Brainketing have evolved and adapted, the impact of artificial intelligence on these disciplines, and the trends and projections that will set the tone for the new digital era.

The Evolutionary Journey of Neuro Marketing: From the Emotional to the Cognitive

✓ **Before the Pandemic: Emotions as Decision Drivers**

Before the global cataclysm, Neuro Marketing was predominantly focused on the study of consumer emotions. Understanding how the brain reacts to specific stimuli made it possible to design strategies that appealed directly to emotions, thus enhancing the connection with the brand. Neuroscience applied to marketing found its niche in the mysterious territory of the human mind.

✓ **After the Pandemic: From the Emotional to the Cognitive**

The pandemic acted as an accelerator of change, leading Neuro Marketing to evolve toward a more holistic understanding of cognitive processing. Beyond emotions, brands began to focus on how consumers process information and make decisions. This ushered in the era of Brainketing, where the interconnection of emotion and cognition became essential to deeply understand the consumer in a post-pandemic environment.

Brainketing and Artificial Intelligence Integration

The Artificial Intelligence Revolution

Artificial intelligence (AI) has been the catalyst for transformation in various industries, and marketing is no exception. Massive data processing capabilities, machine learning and cognitive process simulation have taken Brainketing to new heights. AI becomes the bridge that connects neuroscience with more personalized and effective marketing strategies.

The Impact of AI on Brainketing: Personalization and Prediction

AI powers real-time personalization. By analyzing past and present consumer behavior, brands can instantly tailor their messages, creating unique experiences. In addition, AI's predictive capabilities allow it to anticipate consumer needs and preferences, enabling brands to be proactive rather than reactive.

Trends and Projections in the New Digital Age

Augmented Reality (AR) and Virtual Reality (VR)

Brainketing will benefit greatly from AR and VR. Immersive experiences allow brands to activate specific areas of the brain linked to memory and decision-making. From virtually testing products to engaging in immersive brand narratives, these technologies will push the boundaries of emotional connection.

Brain-Computer Interfaces (BCI)

The direct connection between brain and computer is on the horizon. As more advanced CBIs are developed, brands will be able to understand brain responses in real time, enabling instant adaptation of marketing strategies.

Ethics in Applied Neuroscience

With the increased ability to influence consumer decisions at the brain level, there is a critical need for ethical boundaries. The new digital era will bring with it profound debates about privacy, manipulation and responsibility in the use of neuroscience applied to marketing.

Intersection with Other Sciences and Studies

Consumer Psychology

Consumer psychology merges with Brainketing to understand how psychological factors influence purchasing decisions. The combination of psychological research techniques and neuroscience technologies provides a more complete understanding of consumer behavior.

Anthropology of Consumption

Consumer anthropology becomes crucial to understand how cultural communities interact with Brainketing strategies. Adapting to diverse cultural practices and traditions becomes a vital element for success in the new digital age.

Data Science

Data science and Brainketing form a strategic marriage. The ability to analyze large brain data sets requires a sophisticated data science infrastructure. Accurate interpretation of brain signals becomes a challenge solved by advanced algorithms.

The Neurodigital Landscape of the Future

In the new post-pandemic era, Neuro Marketing and Brainketing are positioned as guiding lights for marketing strategies. The convergence with artificial intelligence, the exploration of new technologies and the intersection with various scientific disciplines open an exciting and challenging landscape.

Ethics will play a key role in the application of these disciplines, and collaboration between scientists, marketers and ethicists will be key to ensuring the responsible use of applied neuroscience. In the end, the ability to understand and respect the mind of the consumer will be the most valuable currency in the neurodigital landscape of the future. We are on the threshold of a revolution where mind and machine intertwine, creating a fascinating scenario where science and marketing converge to transform the way we live and consume.

The Neurodigital Future in Detail: Statistics, Cases and Challenges

Beyond Neuroscience: Data Supporting Evolution

1. Shocking Statistics:

According to a report by consultancy MarketsandMarkets, the neurotechnology market is expected to reach $30.7 billion by 2027, reflecting significant growth since before the pandemic.

Seventy-eight percent of marketers report that they are using or plan to use artificial intelligence technologies in their strategies, according to a Salesforce survey.

2. Success Cases:

Netflix and Brain-Based Recommendations:

The streaming platform uses neuroscience-based algorithms to analyze brain patterns and deliver highly personalized content recommendations. This has led to a 15% increase in user retention.

Neuromarketing in Retail:

Companies like Walmart and Amazon are using neuromarketing to design online shopping experiences that align with the user's cognitive preferences, thereby improving customer satisfaction and increasing conversions.

Artificial Intelligence in Practice: Transforming the Consumer Experience

Real Time Personalization:

AI makes it possible to personalize the consumer experience in real time. Platforms such as Spotify adjust playlists based on the user's brain reactions, improving satisfaction and retention.

2. Cognitive Advertising:

Brands such as Coca-Cola use cognitive ads that adapt according to the viewer's brain responses. This has been shown to increase attention and retention of the advertising message.

Trends That Will Define the Neurodigital Future

Augmented Reality and Virtual Reality (AR/VR):

The AR/VR market is projected to reach $94.4 billion by 2027, according to Allied Market Research. Brands such as IKEA are using these technologies to allow consumers to "try on" products virtually before they buy.

2. Brain-Computer Interfaces (BCI):

Companies such as Elon Musk's Neuralink are working on advanced CBIs that could fundamentally change the way we interact with technology. These interfaces are expected to expand the applications of Brainketing, enabling a deeper understanding of brain responses.

Ethical Challenges and Responsibility in Neuromarketing

Privacy and Consent:

As Brainketing technologies advance, there is a critical need to address privacy issues and obtain informed consent. It is essential to establish sound ethical standards to ensure that the use of applied neuroscience is ethical and transparent.

Cognitive Manipulation:

The risk of cognitive manipulation poses significant ethical challenges. The line between influencing consumer decisions and improper manipulation can be thin. Brands must be aware of the responsibility that comes with accessing the consumer's mind.

Intersection of Sciences: Collaborating for an Integral Perspective

1. Consumer Psychology and Neuroscience:

Collaboration between psychologists and consumer neuroscientists enables a deeper understanding of how purchasing decisions are influenced by emotional and cognitive factors.

2. Anthropology and Brainketing:

Consumer anthropology merges with Brainketing to understand how cultural communities interact with brain-based marketing strategies. This translates into more effective and culturally sensitive campaigns.

3. Data Science and Brain Processing:

Data science facilitates the accurate interpretation of brain signals. Collaboration between data scientists and brain processing experts is essential to achieve significant advances in Brainketing.

The Neurodigital Future with Responsibility and Success

Neuro Marketing and Brainketing are at the epicenter of the digital revolution, shaping the way brands interact with consumers. With shocking statistics supporting their growth, success stories demonstrating their effectiveness and ethical challenges requiring attention, these disciplines are constantly evolving.

The intersection with artificial intelligence, the exploration of new technologies and collaboration with various scientific disciplines open the door to an exciting and challenging landscape. As we navigate this uncharted territory, responsibility and ethics become essential compasses to ensure proper use of these tools that have the power to penetrate the human mind.

The neurodigital future promises a deeper connection between brands and consumers, but this journey must be undertaken with caution and a deep understanding of the ethical responsibilities involved. Science and marketing are converging in a symphonic dance that will transform the way we live, consume and understand the complexity of the human mind.

Neuro Marketing and Brainketing: The Expert Perspective on the Digital Future

To delve into the future of the disciplines of Neuro Marketing and Brainketing, it is crucial to analyze the visions of experts and scholars who have contributed significantly to these areas.

Neuro Marketing: Understanding Consumer Emotions

Antonio Damasio:

Damasio, renowned neurologist and author of Descartes' Error, highlights the direct connection between emotions and decision making. His pioneering research reveals how rational decisions are intrinsically linked to emotions, providing crucial foundations for the emotional approach to Neuro Marketing.

Gerald Zaltman:

Zaltman, a professor at Harvard Business School, is known for his work in neuromarketing research. His "ZMET" technique (Zaltman Metaphor Elicitation Technique) uses neuroscience to reveal consumers' unconscious perceptions, providing valuable insights into the factors that influence purchasing decisions.

Martin Lindstrom:

Lindstrom, author of "Buyology: Truths and Lies About Why We Buy," discusses how the brain reacts to marketing stimuli. His work highlights the importance of understanding neurological responses to develop more effective marketing strategies.

Brainketing: Integrating Cognition and Emotion

1. Patrick Renvoise and Christophe Morin:

The authors of "Neuromarketing: Understanding the Buy Buttons in Your Customer's Brain" are leaders in the transition to Brainketing. Their approach combines neuroscience and psychology to understand not only emotions, but also the cognitive processes that influence buying decisions.

2. Roger Dooley:

Dooley, author of "Brainfluence: 100 Ways to Persuade and Convince Consumers with Neuromarketing," highlights how understanding cognitive processes can be leveraged to influence consumer decisions. His work highlights the need to integrate cognition into marketing strategies.

Clear Definitions for a Clairvoyant Future

Neuro Marketing:

Neuro Marketing is defined as the application of neuroscience techniques and methodologies to the field of marketing. Its main objective is to understand how consumers' brains respond to marketing stimuli, focusing initially on emotions to predict and enhance purchasing decisions.

2. Brainketing:

Brainketing, an evolution of Neuro Marketing, expands to encompass both emotions and cognitive processes. It goes beyond understanding emotional reactions by exploring how the brain processes information and makes decisions. The term reflects the integration of strategies based on whole brain activity.

The Future: Integration, Ethics and Technological Advances

1. Dr. Thomas Ramsøy:

Ramsøy, neuroscience expert and author of "Introduction to Neuromarketing & Consumer Neuroscience", highlights the need for closer integration between neuroscience and technology for a successful future of Neuromarketing. His approach emphasizes the crucial role of ethics in the application of these disciplines.

2. Dr. Reid Montague:

Montague, a neuroscientist and author of "Your Brain Is (Almost) Perfect: How We Make Decisions," provides insights into decision making. His work highlights how a deep understanding of brain processes can lead to significant advances in personalizing and tailoring marketing strategies.

The future of these disciplines will be forged by collaboration between neuroscientists, marketing experts and ethicists. As we move into an era where technology and the mind are intertwined, the wisdom of these scholars will act as a beacon, guiding us toward ethical practices, effective strategies and a deeper understanding of the consumer in the new digital age.

Current and Future Perspectives: Neuro Marketing, Brainketing and the Digital Revolution

Neuro Marketing Today: Understanding Emotions

1. Dr. Gemma Calvert:

Calvert, neuroscientist and founder of Neurosense, highlights the application of Neuro Marketing in improving the customer experience. Her approach focuses on how emotions can influence customer loyalty, and advocates for a deeper understanding of the emotional connection in marketing strategies.

2. Dr. Beau Lotto:

Lotto, a neuroscientist and co-founder of Lab of Misfits Studio, explores perception and decision-making. His work highlights how brands can leverage brain plasticity to create memorable experiences. Adaptability in Neuro Marketing strategy becomes crucial to stay relevant.

Brainketing and Cognitive Integration: Towards Informed Decisions

1. Dr. A.K. Pradeep:

Pradeep, founder and CEO of NeuroFocus, discusses the evolution towards Brainketing, highlighting the need to understand cognition. His research highlights the importance of combining emotion with cognition to create more effective, consumer-centric marketing strategies.

2. Dr. Christophe Morin:

Morin, co-author of "The Persuasion Code," highlights the practical application of Brainketing in consumer decision making. His approach focuses on how brands can influence both emotions and cognition to achieve optimal results. Adapting to this holistic approach is essential for future success.

The Ethical Challenge and Responsibility in Technological Advancement

1. Dr. Nathalie Nahai:

Nahai, a web psychologist and author of "Webs of Influence," highlights the need to address ethical challenges in the application of these disciplines. Her work focuses on how brands can use neuroscience ethically, avoiding manipulation and respecting consumer privacy.

2. Prof. Rafael Ramirez:

Ramirez, an expert in business ethics, stresses the importance of establishing clear ethical standards in the application of neuroscience in marketing. His focus is on corporate responsibility and how brands can lead with integrity in the era of Neuro Marketing and Brainketing.

The Future: Convergence, Innovation and Collaboration

1. Dr. Moran Cerf:

Cerf, a neuroscientist and marketing professor, highlights the continuing convergence between neuroscience and marketing. His vision focuses on how technological innovation will enable an even deeper understanding of the consumer mind. Interdisciplinary collaboration becomes essential to drive future research.

2. Dr. Elissa Moses:

Moses, neuroscientist and founder of Emotiv Research, addresses the need for further progress in understanding brain complexities. Her work highlights how continued innovation in brain measurement technology will open up new opportunities for Neuro Marketing and Brainketing in the next decade.

Collaboration between researchers, ethicists and marketers is essential to successfully navigate the future of these disciplines. As we move toward a landscape where technology and neuroscience converge, these current and future perspectives will act as essential guides to harnessing the transformative potential of Neuro Marketing and Brainketing in the digital age.

The Continuing Evolution of Neuromarketing: Today's Relevance

Technological Advances: The New Frontier of Neuromarketing

Today, technological advances have catapulted neuromarketing to a position of increased relevance. The introduction of techniques such as functional magnetic resonance imaging (fMRI) and electroencephalography (EEG) has enabled marketers to explore brain responses in a more detailed and precise manner. These high-tech tools have redefined how we understand and apply marketing strategies.

Practical Example:

Companies such as Nielsen Consumer Neuroscience have adopted advanced technologies to measure consumers' emotional and cognitive response to advertising stimuli. This approach not only provides richer data, but also allows strategies to be adjusted in real time.

Consumer Neuroscience: Beyond Emotions

The evolution of neuromarketing has led to a deeper understanding of consumer neuroscience. While emotions remain central, the discipline has expanded to encompass cognitive processes. This involves considering how information is processed and retained in the consumer's brain.

Importance in Practice:

Neuromarketing strategies now seek not only to generate positive emotions, but also to facilitate a clearer understanding of the advertising message. Techniques are being developed to optimize information retention and decision making based on brain processing.

Personalization and Customer Experience: Keys to Success

With the evolution of neuromarketing, personalization has become a crucial component. Companies seek to understand individual consumer preferences at a deeper level, using brain data to tailor strategies and products more precisely.

Meaningful Application:

Platforms like Amazon use neuroscience-based algorithms to personalize product recommendations, creating shopping experiences highly tailored to each user's tastes and preferences.

Emphasis on Ethics and Transparency: A Major Turnaround

As neuromarketing has gained ground, there has also been an increased awareness of ethics and transparency in its application. The responsibility of brands to use brain data ethically has become imperative, with a focus on building consumer trust.

Important Development:

Neuromarketing organizations and experts are collaborating to establish clear ethical standards. Transparency in the collection and use of brain data has become a key differentiator for companies looking to build long-term relationships with their customers.

The Crucial Role in Business Decision Making

The evolution of neuromarketing has not only transformed marketing strategies, but also plays a crucial role in business decision making. Companies are integrating brain data into their market analysis and strategic plans, using these insights to anticipate trends and opportunities.

Real Impact:

Leading companies in a variety of industries are adopting neuroscience-based approaches to product development, innovation and strategic planning. This not only allows them to stay ahead of the curve, but also to respond nimbly to changing market dynamics.

Neuromarketing as a Transformational Tool

The continuous evolution of neuromarketing has elevated it from a novel tool to an essential component in the arsenal of modern marketing strategies. Its ability to provide deep insights, personalize experiences and ethically approach brain data collection positions it as a key enabler in the current and future digital era. Companies that embrace and fully understand this emerging discipline are better equipped to navigate the complex contemporary marketing landscape.

Brainketing: The Cognitive Frontiers of Marketing

The Transition to Brainketing: A Revolution in Marketing Strategy

The evolution of Brainketing represents a significant transition in marketing strategy. While Neuromarketing initially focused on emotional responses, Brainketing broadens this perspective by integrating cognitive processes. This holistic approach seeks to understand not only how consumers feel, but also how they think.

Example Transformer:

Companies like Google are adopting Brainketing approaches to better understand the thought processes behind online searches. This not only improves the relevance of results, but also enables deeper personalization.

Focus on Cognition: Beyond Pure Emotions

Brainketing recognizes that purchasing decisions are not only based on emotions, but also on thought processes and reasoning. By understanding how the consumer's brain processes information, marketing strategies can be tailored to influence not only emotions, but also rational decision making.

Current Meaning:

Companies such as IBM are using Brainketing techniques to understand how customers process technical information and how this processing affects their purchasing decisions in the business technology arena.

Adapting to Cognitive Personalization: Beyond Emotional Preferences

The importance of Brainketing lies in its ability to offer deeper personalization, considering not only emotional preferences, but also cognitive preferences. By analyzing how customers process information, companies can tailor messages and experiences more precisely.

Featured Application:

Streaming platforms like Netflix use Brainketing strategies to analyze viewing patterns, understand how users process information about movies and shows, and tailor recommendations accordingly.

Ethics and Responsibility: A Fundamental Pillar in Brainketing

Brainketing has also generated increased attention on ethics and accountability in the use of cognitive data. Transparency in how this data is collected and used has become a priority, and companies are taking steps to ensure the privacy and confidentiality of brain information.

Ethical Development:

Organizations such as the Neuroethics Society are leading the conversation about the ethical challenges associated with Brainketing. Establishing sound ethical practices is essential to gaining consumer trust and maintaining integrity in the application of these strategies.

Business Integration and Strategic Decision Making

Brainketing not only transforms marketing strategies, but also influences business decision making at deeper levels. Companies are using cognitive data to understand how customers perceive their products, how they make decisions and how these perceptions affect business strategy.

Impact on Companies:

Companies such as Apple have integrated brainketing approaches into product development, evaluating how consumers perceive and process information about technological innovations before bringing new products to market.

Brainketing as a Business Transformation Engine

Today, Brainketing is emerging as a driver of transformation in business and marketing strategy. Its ability to understand both emotions and cognitive processes allows for deeper personalization and more tailored strategies. Ethics and transparency are essential pillars in the effective application of Brainketing, ensuring that the cognitive revolution in marketing is conducted responsibly and respectfully. Companies that fully embrace this evolution are better positioned to lead in the complex and dynamic world of contemporary marketing.

Future Perspectives in Neuromarketing and Brainketing: Navigating the New Cognitive Marketing Era

Integrating Emotion and Cognition for Holistic Marketing

In this journey through the evolution of Neuromarketing and the rise of Brainketing, we have witnessed how these disciplines have transformed from emotion-focused approaches to strategies that embrace both emotion and cognition. The merging of these dimensions has driven a more complete understanding of the consumer mind.

Key Aspects:

Integral Personalization: The ability to personalize experiences based on emotions and cognitive processes has emerged as a powerful tool.

Ethics and Transparency: Emphasis on ethics and transparency in the application of these disciplines has become imperative to gain consumer confidence.

Business Integration: Neuromarketing and Brainketing not only impact marketing strategies, but also influence business decision making, from product development to strategic planning.

Recommendations for Neuromarketing Professionals: Navigating the New Cognitive Reality

For Neuromarketing and Brainketing professionals, some key recommendations emerge:

Continuous Updating: Keeping abreast of the latest research and advances in neuroscience and technology is essential to apply up-to-date and effective approaches.

Emphasis on Ethics: Prioritizing ethics in the collection and application of brain data is critical. Establishing clear ethical standards will strengthen the integrity of the strategies implemented.

Complementary Skills Development: Integrating skills in related areas such as artificial intelligence, data analysis and business ethics can enhance the ability to effectively apply Neuromarketing and Brainketing.

The Cognitive Revolution in Marketing and its Global Projection

The cognitive revolution in marketing, spearheaded by Neuromarketing and Brainketing, is not simply a paradigm shift; it is a fundamental transformation that redefines how we understand, approach and connect with consumers. This impact is not limited to one industry or region, but spans the global marketing landscape.

World Overview:

From Silicon Valley to emerging cities in Asia, the application of these disciplines is shaping the future of marketing. The adaptability of cognitive strategies is becoming essential to meet the diverse needs and expectations of global audiences.

Challenges to overcome:

While the cognitive revolution promises unparalleled opportunities, we face critical challenges in terms of privacy, regulations and the need for broader education about these disciplines.

Impacting Future Vision:

Looking ahead, the convergence of artificial intelligence, neuroscience and marketing points to a future where consumer experiences will be defined by deeper, more authentic insights. Accurate prediction of consumer trends and desires will be an achievable reality.

Conclusion Shocking:

In this dawn of the cognitive era, collaboration between scientists, marketers and ethicists is essential. Only through this union can we fully harness the potential of Neuromarketing and Brainketing to not only influence purchasing decisions, but also to genuinely improve the lives of consumers in an increasingly digital and cognitive world. The revolution is just beginning, and the marketing narrative of the future is being written in the complexities of the human mind and the intersection with technology.

Neuromarketing vs. Brainketing: A Comparative Analysis and Post-Pandemic Impact

Differences and Coincidences: Unraveling Cognitive Dimensions.

Neuromarketing: Focusing on Emotions

1. Primary Approach:

Neuromarketing: Focused on understanding the consumer's emotional responses through neuroscience, prioritizing the emotional connection with the brand.

2. Key Tools:

Neuromarketing: Uses techniques such as functional magnetic resonance imaging (fMRI) and measurement of electrical brain activity (EEG) to analyze brain activity related to emotions.

3. Typical Applications:

Neuromarketing: Strategies to generate positive emotional responses to products or services, improving the emotional connection with the brand.

Brainketing: Integration of Emotion and Cognition

1. Primary Approach:

Brainketing: Broadens the Neuromarketing perspective by integrating both emotional and cognitive processes, recognizing the importance of both in consumer decision making.

2. Key Tools:

Brainketing: Uses Neuromarketing tools but with an additional focus on analyzing how the brain processes information and makes decisions.

3. Typical Applications:

Brainketing: Strategies that not only seek to generate positive emotions, but also to understand how consumers process information to influence more informed decisions.

Meeting Points in the Cognitive Revolution

Advanced Technology Integration:

Both approaches make use of advanced technology, such as magnetic resonance imaging and electroencephalography, to obtain detailed data on brain activity.

Ethical Adaptation:

Both Neuromarketing and Brainketing recognize the importance of ethics in the collection and application of brain data, seeking to establish clear ethical standards.

Focus on Personalization:

Both seek to customize strategies and experiences to suit consumers' individual preferences and thought processes.

Post-Pandemic Impact: Adaptation and Challenges

Neuromarketing After the Pandemic:

Adaptation: The need for emotional connection intensified during the pandemic, and Neuromarketing has evolved to address the changing emotional dynamics of consumers.

Challenges: Restrictions on physical interaction have challenged strategies focused on face-to-face emotional experiences, requiring adaptation to digital strategies.

Brainketing After the Pandemic:

Adaptation: The inclusion of cognitive processes in Brainketing has enabled a more effective adaptation to the need to understand and influence consumers' informed decisions.

Challenges: The saturation of digital information has required more precise strategies to stand out in the consumer's mind, demanding a more detailed focus on how information is processed.

Future: Which Has the Most Potential?

Both Neuromarketing and Brainketing have a crucial role to play in the future of marketing, but Brainketing's potential is broader because of its holistic approach. The ability to understand both emotions and cognition provides a strategic advantage, especially in a world where consumers are seeking richer, more informed experiences.

The evolution toward Brainketing reflects a more complete understanding of the consumer's mind and superior adaptability to today's challenges. However, success will depend on the ability of professionals to balance emotional connection with cognitive influence ethically and effectively. The cognitive revolution in marketing is underway, and the future belongs to those who navigate this intersection of emotion and cognition masterfully.

The Cognitive Frontiers of Marketing

The revolution in marketing strategy, driven by Neuromarketing and elevated to new heights by Brainketing, has taken us to the very frontiers of the consumer mind. While Neuromarketing allowed us to dive into the emotional waters, Brainketing takes us further into the intricate thought processes and informed decisions.

Future Outlook: Where Does True Potential Lie?

The future potential lies in the harmonious integration of emotions and cognition, and this is where Brainketing excels. In a post-pandemic world, where digitalization has accelerated transformation, understanding how consumers process information becomes vital.

Adaptability in the Digital World: Brainketing as a Shining Beacon

Brainketing, recognizing the need to adapt to saturated digital environments, stands as a shining beacon. Its ability to not only generate emotional connections, but also influence decisions based on critical thinking, positions it as the next frontier in the evolution of marketing.

Challenges and Opportunities: The Balanced Dance of Ethics and Effectiveness.

The future also poses ethical challenges. Brain data collection demands clear ethical standards and transparency. Those who manage to balance emotional connection and cognitive influence in an ethical manner will be the undisputed leaders in this new paradigm.

Invitation to the Master's Program: Navigating the Cognitive Revolution

At the crossroads of emotions and thoughts, I invite marketers to perfect their mastery of Brainketing. Here, the consumer narrative is not only felt, but also understood and shaped through cognitive science.

The cognitive revolution in marketing is in full swing, and those who embrace the duality of emotion and cognition will be at the forefront of the next era. The journey is just beginning, and the mind of the consumer is the compass that will guide the brave into uncharted territory of authentic connections and informed decisions. May this revolution be remembered not only for transforming marketing, but for creating experiences that resonate deep in the mind of the consumer, transcending the mere transaction to become a lasting and meaningful relationship.

Neuro Marketing and Brainketing: Navigating the Frontiers of the Mind After the Pandemic

The marketing world has witnessed an unprecedented transformation in recent decades, and Neuro Marketing has emerged as a fundamental discipline that has given way to an even more profound evolution: Brainketing. In this article, we will explore the evolution of these disciplines, their post-pandemic adaptation and the impact they have had in different regions of the world, identifying the areas with the greatest growth potential.

Neuro Marketing: An Overview of its Evolution and Adaptation

From Emotions to Cognition: The Transformation of Neuro Marketing

Neuro Marketing has been a pioneer in understanding consumer emotions through advanced techniques such as functional magnetic resonance imaging and electroencephalography. However, its evolution towards Brainketing has broadened its scope, incorporating not only emotional responses, but also the cognitive processes that influence purchasing decisions.

Post-Pandemic Adaptation: The Need for Connection in a Digitized World

The pandemic has accelerated digitization and changed the dynamics of interaction. Neuro Marketing, by focusing on emotional connection, has had to adapt to maintain its relevance in a world where physical interaction has become limited. More digital strategies, based on a deep understanding of emotions expressed in virtual environments, have emerged as key responses.

Brainketing: The Fusion of Emotion and Cognition

Beyond Neuro Marketing: Integrating Cognitive Processes

Brainketing represents the natural evolution of Neuro Marketing by embracing both emotions and cognitive processes. It recognizes that consumer decision making is not simply emotional, but also involves rational evaluation of information. This integration provides a more complete and accurate view of consumer behavior.

Post-Pandemic Adaptation: The Cognitive Comprehension Advantage

In a post-pandemic world where information is overwhelming, Brainketing has proven to be more adaptable by focusing on how consumers process information. The ability to influence not only emotions, but also decisions based on critical thinking, has become an invaluable asset.

Impact in World Regions: Identifying Growth Potentials

North America: Leading Adoption and Development

North America has been a leader in the adoption and development of Neuro Marketing and Brainketing techniques. Companies in Silicon Valley and other key regions have led the way in integrating these disciplines into their marketing strategies.

Europe: Sustained Growth with an Emphasis on Ethics

In Europe, growth has been steady, with a particular emphasis on the ethics of brain data collection. Countries such as Germany and the United Kingdom have led the way in establishing clear ethical standards to guide the application of these disciplines.

Asia: Explosive Potential and Rapid Digital Adaptation

Asia, with its rapid adaptation to digital technologies, has experienced an explosive potential in the application of Neuro Marketing and Brainketing. Countries such as China and Japan have led the way in the implementation of strategies based on a deep understanding of emotions and cognitive processes.

Latin America: Emerging Growth with Unique Challenges

Latin America has experienced emerging growth, albeit with unique challenges. Cultural diversity and differences in technology adoption present challenges, but also opportunities to customize strategies to each country's particularities.

Africa: Exploring New Horizons

In Africa, Neuro Marketing and Brainketing applications are beginning to explore new horizons. Although growth is slower compared to other regions, progressive adaptation to digital technologies suggests potential as connectivity increases.

Asia Pacific Perspectives: Leading the Way in Innovation

Asia Pacific is leading innovation in the use of Neuro Marketing and Brainketing. Australia, Singapore and New Zealand are rapidly adopting these disciplines, leveraging the emotional and cognitive connection to drive effective marketing strategies.

Projected Growth in Latin American, Asian and African Countries: Challenges and Opportunities

Latin America: Connectivity and Culturally Responsive Challenges

In Latin America, projected growth faces challenges of connectivity and a culturally receptive but diverse population. Overcoming these barriers will require customized strategies, taking into account differences in technology adoption and emotional response to marketing campaigns.

Asia: Opportunities in Cultural Diversity

In Asia, especially in lesser-known countries such as Vietnam and the Philippines, opportunities lie in cultural diversity. Strategies that respect and embrace cultural differences have the potential to earn consumer trust and generate stronger connections.

Africa: Gradual Growth with Promising Prospects

In Africa, growth is gradual but with promising prospects. As connectivity improves and adoption of digital technologies increases, Neuro Marketing and Brainketing applications can play a crucial role in creating more effective and relevant campaigns.

In the Global Consumer Mindset

The evolution from Neuro Marketing to Brainketing has marked a milestone in consumer understanding, but its effective application varies in different regions of the world. North America leads in adoption, Europe excels in ethics, Asia experiences explosive growth, Latin America faces unique challenges, Africa explores new frontiers, and Asia Pacific leads in innovation.

The potential for growth in Latin American, non-familiar Asian and African countries lies in adapting strategies to the cultural diversity and unique characteristics of each region. Overcoming connectivity challenges, respecting cultural differences and leveraging the rapid adoption of digital technologies are key to future success.

The marketing of the future is not only about understanding consumer emotions, but also about understanding the complexity of their cognitive processes. In a post-pandemic world, the ability to connect emotionally and influence rationally will define the success of global marketing strategies. Navigating the mind of the global consumer is an exciting challenge, and those who masterfully embrace it will be at the forefront of the next era of global marketing.

Latin America: Unique Challenges and Opportunities

Connectivity Challenges:

Latin America presents significant challenges in terms of connectivity, especially in rural areas. To leverage the potential of Neuro Marketing and Brainketing, it is essential to address these gaps by promoting initiatives that improve the digital infrastructure.

Cultural Diversity:

The rich cultural diversity in Latin America requires a strategic approach. Campaigns must be carefully tailored to resonate with the specific emotions and values of each country. Strategies that embrace local cultural identity will have more impact.

Variable Technology Adoption:

Although the adoption of digital technologies is increasing, there is significant variability among Latin American countries. Strategies that take into account these differences, such as the prevalent use of mobile devices in some countries, will be more effective.

Growth Projection:

Despite the challenges, Latin America offers exciting opportunities. With improving connectivity and an increasingly digital youth population, the projection for growth is positive. Brainketing strategies that adapt to cultural diversity and promote emotional connection will resonate especially well.

Asia: Exploring Beyond the Known Powers

Opportunities in Lesser Known Countries:

In Asia, lesser-known countries such as Vietnam, the Philippines and Malaysia are experiencing an increase in the adoption of digital technologies. Opportunities lie in exploring these emerging markets and adapting Neuro Marketing and Brainketing strategies to unique cultural characteristics.

Respect for Cultural Diversity:

Asia, with its vast cultural diversity, demands a deep respect for differences. Strategies that dive into the richness of local culture, avoiding generalizations, will build the authenticity needed to connect with consumers on a deeper level.

Innovation in Technology:

Asia leads the way in technology innovation and is rapidly adopting new platforms and applications. Brainketing strategies can capitalize on this innovation, taking advantage of the region's specific technology preferences.

Growth Projection:

The growth projection in Asia remains positive. Rapid adaptation to technology and a growing middle class provide fertile ground for strategies that combine emotional connection with cognitive understanding.

Africa: Gradual Challenges with Promising Prospects

Evolving Connectivity:

Africa has experienced challenges in connectivity, but a gradual evolution can be observed. Initiatives that promote digital infrastructure, such as broadband expansion, will be crucial to unlock the potential of Neuro Marketing and Brainketing.

Cultural Diversity on the Rise:

Cultural diversity in Africa is a valuable asset. Strategies that embrace this diversity, recognizing the particularities of each region and country, will be more effective in building meaningful connections.

Growth of Mobile Technologies:

The growth of mobile technology adoption in Africa offers opportunities. Strategies focused on mobile devices and applications can more effectively reach a diverse audience.

Growth Projection:

Although growth is gradual, the outlook is promising. Young demographics and increased connectivity suggest that Africa is on an upward path in the application of Neuro Marketing and Brainketing.

Asia Pacific: Leading the Innovation Revolution

Continuous Innovation:

Asia Pacific, with countries such as Australia, Singapore and New Zealand, is leading the innovation revolution. The adoption of cutting-edge technologies and progressive mindset make this region a fertile ground for advanced Neuro Marketing and Brainketing strategies.

Emphasis on Consumer Experience:

The region places a strong emphasis on consumer experience. Strategies that focus not just on selling, but on building memorable experiences, will resonate with consumers in Asia Pacific.

Adaptation to New Platforms:

Rapid adaptation to new platforms and technologies offers opportunities for experimentation and innovation. Strategies that anticipate emerging trends will find fertile ground for growth.

Growth Projection:

The growth projection in Asia Pacific remains strong. The combination of technological innovation and a consumer-centric approach places the region at the forefront of the Neuro Marketing and Brainketing revolution.

A World Connected by the Mind of the Consumer

In a post-pandemic world, Neuro Marketing and Brainketing have evolved to be the key tools in connecting with the mind of the consumer globally. Latin America faces challenges of connectivity and cultural diversity, but offers exciting potential. Asia, including lesser-known countries, is leading innovation and experiencing explosive growth. Africa, with gradual challenges, has promising prospects as connectivity improves. Asia Pacific is leading the innovation revolution, with solid growth projections.

The Successful Use of Neuromarketing and Brainketing by Sectors and Companies in the World

Neuromarketing and Brainketing have become powerful tools to understand and connect with consumers at deeper levels. Various economic sectors and leading companies around the world have adopted these disciplines to optimize their marketing strategies. Below is an analysis by region and major countries.

North America: Leaders in Technology and Entertainment

Technology: Apple Inc.

Approach: Apple has used Neuromarketing to understand consumers' emotional responses to its products. From packaging design to advertising campaigns, the company has integrated strategies based on emotional and cognitive connection.

2. Entertainment: Netflix

Approach: Netflix has implemented Brainketing techniques to personalize content recommendations. Its algorithm uses neuroscientific data to understand individual preferences and deliver highly personalized viewing experiences.

Europe: Emphasis on Ethics and User Experience

Automotive: Mercedes-Benz

Approach: Mercedes-Benz has used Neuromarketing to design driving experiences that align with consumers' emotions and expectations. The company has applied techniques to understand brain response during interaction with its vehicles.

Fashion: Zara (Inditex)

Focus: Zara, part of the Inditex group, has integrated Brainketing strategies to personalize the shopping experience in physical and online stores. Neuroscientific analysis is used to improve store design and optimize product presentation.

3. Sustainable Tourism: TUI Group (Germany/United Kingdom/France)

Approach: TUI Group has integrated neuromarketing techniques to understand travelers' emotions and expectations. Neuroscience research has influenced sustainable destination promotion strategies in Germany, the UK and France.

4. Ethical Fashion: H&M Conscious Collection (Sweden/Germany/Italy/France)

Approach: H&M's Conscious Collection line has applied Brainketing to communicate its commitment to ethical and sustainable fashion. The neuroscience-based emotional connection has been central to marketing strategies in Sweden, Germany, Italy and France.

5. Ethical Financial Technology: Triodos Bank (Netherlands/Belgium/Spain/Germany)

Approach: Triodos Bank has explored Neuromarketing and Brainketing techniques to communicate its ethical financial services. Neuroscientific adaptation has influenced marketing strategies and value-aligned image building in the Netherlands, Belgium, Spain and Germany.

Asia: Technological Innovation and Rapid Adaptation

1. Technology: Samsung Electronics (South Korea)

Approach: Samsung has applied Neuromarketing techniques to understand consumer preferences and improve the usability of its electronic products. Neuroscience research has influenced the design of interfaces and product features.

2. E-commerce: Alibaba Group (China)

Approach: Alibaba has used Brainketing to personalize the shopping experience on its platform. Neuroscience-based artificial intelligence (AI) is applied to analyze shopping patterns and deliver highly relevant recommendations.

Africa: Exploring New Horizons

1. Telecommunications: MTN Group (South Africa)

Approach: MTN Group has adopted Neuromarketing techniques to understand consumers' emotional responses to telecommunications services. Neuroscientific research has influenced advertising campaigns and loyalty strategies.

2. Tourism: Kenya Airways (Kenya)

Approach: Kenya Airways has explored Brainketing to personalize the travel experience. Neuroscientific understanding of passenger expectations and emotions has influenced service improvement and destination promotion.

Asia Pacific: Innovation and Consumer Experience

Technology: Sony Corporation (Japan)

Approach: Sony has integrated neuromarketing strategies into the development of technology products. Neuroscience research has informed aspects such as ergonomic design and user interface.

2. Retail: Woolworths Group (Australia)

Approach: Woolworths has applied Brainketing techniques to improve the shopping experience in its stores. Personalization based on neuroscientific data has influenced product layout and customized promotions.

3. Innovative Technology: Xiaomi (China/India/Europe)

Approach: Xiaomi has integrated neuromarketing into its strategy to understand consumer preferences for technology products. The application of neuroscientific principles has influenced launch strategies and improved user experience in China, India and Europe.

4. Personalized Food: Yum China (China/Asia Pacific)

Focus: Yum China, owner of brands such as KFC and Pizza Hut, has applied Brainketing techniques to personalize food offerings. The neuroscience-based emotional connection has been key to product presentation and marketing strategies in China and other Asia Pacific countries.

5. Emotional Entertainment: BTS (South Korea/Global)

Approach: BTS brand management has explored Neuromarketing to understand the emotions and expectations of their fans globally. Neuroscientific research has influenced promotional strategies and the construction of emotional experiences in South Korea and globally.

Latin America: Emerging Development with Growing Potential

1. Communications and Entertainment: América Móvil (Mexico)

Focus: América Móvil, through brands such as Telcel and Claro, has applied neuromarketing to understand user preferences and behaviors in communications and entertainment services. Neuroscientific research has influenced advertising strategies and service development.

2. Mass Consumption: Alicorp (Peru)

Approach: Alicorp, a food and consumer products company in Peru, has explored Brainketing to understand consumers' emotional reactions to its products. The application of neuroscientific techniques has contributed to the improvement of packaging and positioning strategies in the Peruvian market.

3. Energy: Petrobras (Brazil)

Approach: Petrobras has integrated Neuromarketing to effectively communicate energy-related initiatives and messages. Understanding emotional responses has been key in awareness campaigns and positioning strategies in Brazil.

4. Financial Technology: Nubank (Brazil)

Focus: Nubank, a financial technology company in Brazil, has used Brainketing techniques to personalize the user experience in its digital financial services. Neuroscientific adaptation has influenced user interface and customer retention strategies.

5. Tourism: Despegar.com (Argentina)

Focus: Despegar.com, a travel technology company in Argentina, has explored Neuromarketing to understand travelers' emotions and expectations. Neuroscientific research has informed promotional strategies and user experience design.

6. Sustainable Fashion: TAL Cual (Chile)

Approach: TAL Cual, a Chilean sustainable fashion brand, has integrated Brainketing strategies to communicate the ethical and environmental values of its products. The emotional connection based on neuroscience has been fundamental in the construction of a conscious and attractive brand.

7. E-Commerce: MercadoLibre (Argentina/Brazil/Mexico)

Focus: MercadoLibre, an e-commerce platform present in several Latin American countries, has applied Neuromarketing and Brainketing techniques to personalize the online shopping experience. Adaptation to individual preferences has influenced the effectiveness of product recommendations and loyalty strategies.

Africa: Exploration and Cultural Awareness

Africa, with its cultural and geographic diversity, is exploring Neuromarketing and Brainketing to generate cultural awareness and adapt strategies to its unique contexts.

1. African Fashion: MaXhosa (South Africa/Global)

Approach: MaXhosa, a South African fashion brand, has integrated Neuromarketing techniques to communicate its Xhosa-inspired designs. The neuroscience-based emotional connection has been key to marketing strategies in South Africa and globally.

2. Cultural Tourism: Magical Kenya (Kenya/Africa)

Approach: The "Magical Kenya" campaign has explored Brainketing to promote tourism destinations based on the rich cultural diversity of Kenya and Africa. Neuroscientific understanding has informed promotional strategies and cultural awareness.

3. Sustainable Technology: M-Pesa (Kenya/Tanzania/South Africa/Africa)

Approach: M-Pesa, a mobile payment service, has applied Neuromarketing and Brainketing techniques to communicate its impact on financial inclusion and sustainability. Neuroscientific adaptation has influenced marketing strategies in Kenya, Tanzania, South Africa and other African countries.

Oceania: Nature and User Experience

Oceania, with its natural beauty and focus on user experience, has incorporated Neuromarketing and Brainketing to effectively connect with consumers.

1. Sustainable Tourism: Tourism Australia (Australia/Global)

Approach: Tourism Australia has integrated neuromarketing techniques to promote tourist destinations based on the country's natural beauty. The neuroscience-based emotional connection has been key in national and international promotion strategies.

2. Sustainable Fashion: Outland Denim (Australia/Global)

Focus: Outland Denim, an Australian sustainable fashion brand, has applied Brainketing to communicate its ethical commitment. Neuroscientific insights have influenced marketing strategies in Australia and globally.

An Emotionally United World

Neuromarketing and Brainketing, as they are adopted across continents and regions, reveal an emotionally connected world. From personalization strategies in Asia to promoting cultural diversity in Africa, these disciplines are shaping the way brands connect with their audiences globally.

The role of neuroscience in marketing has not only improved the effectiveness of strategies, but has also highlighted the importance of understanding and respecting cultural differences. As companies continue to explore and apply these disciplines, expect further evolution in emotionally connecting with consumers in an increasingly interconnected world.

Connected by Emotions

The global evolution of Neuromarketing and Brainketing has marked a fundamental shift in the way brands relate to consumers. From ethical adaptation in Europe to cultural exploration in Africa, these disciplines have transcended borders, emotionally connecting brands with diverse audiences around the world.

Analysis of the strategies implemented on different continents reveals a common trend: the search for a deeper and more authentic connection with consumers. The application of neuroscience in marketing has allowed not only to better understand motivations and emotions, but also to adapt to unique cultural and economic contexts.

Challenges and Opportunities

As we move into the future, there are both challenges and exciting opportunities for brands and marketers. Some final conclusions are highlighted here:

1. Ethics and Privacy Challenge:

With the increasing reliance on neuroscience in marketing, the ethical handling of consumer data and privacy becomes essential. Brands must be transparent in their approach and ensure data protection.

2. Adaptation to Emerging Technology:

The constant advancement of technology, including artificial intelligence, offers new tools to enhance Neuromarketing strategies. The ability to adapt to these emerging technologies will be crucial to remain relevant.

3. Cultural Inclusiveness:

Respect and understanding of cultural diversity is imperative. Neuromarketing and Brainketing strategies must be flexible and adaptable to resonate with audiences from different cultural backgrounds.

4. Sustainability and Social Responsibility:

Sustainability and social responsibility are central themes. Brands that integrate ethical and sustainable principles into their strategies will gain the trust of conscious consumers.

Future Projections: More Human and Connected Marketing

The future of Neuromarketing and Brainketing is shaping up to be more human and connected marketing. Greater personalization is expected, where brands not only anticipate consumer needs, but also adapt to their values and emotions.

Artificial intelligence will continue to play a crucial role, providing deeper insights and boosting personalization capabilities. However, authenticity and emotional connection will remain the cornerstone of marketing success in the future.

New Horizons: Overcoming Challenges with Creativity and Empathy

On the road to new horizons, creativity and empathy will be the most powerful tools. Overcoming ethical challenges, adapting to technology and embracing cultural diversity will require an innovative approach and a deep understanding of consumer psychology.

Neuromarketing and Brainketing, as they evolve in response to changing global market dynamics, are opening the door to a future where brands not only sell products, but also build lasting emotional experiences. In this journey toward emotional connection, brands that embrace authenticity and empathy will be at the forefront of the marketing revolution, leading a movement toward a more human and connected world.

EPILOG

A New Dawn in Marketing and Sales

As we close the pages of "The Power of Adaptation: Marketing, Sales and the Age of Artificial Intelligence," we bid farewell to an exciting journey through transformation, innovation and resilience in the world of marketing and sales. We explored post-pandemic challenges, dismantled entrenched myths and embraced the silent revolution of artificial intelligence.

In this epilogue, we reflect on the journey we undertook together and how we have witnessed the evolution of strategies that stand the test of time.

Adaptation, that powerful catalyst for change, takes center stage in this story. We have plunged into the turbulent waters of neuromarketing, explored the nooks and crannies of brainketing and bravely faced the uncertainties of the new reality.

As we look to the future, we recognize that marketing and sales have reached a new horizon, driven by artificial intelligence. The ability to adapt to an ever-changing environment has become the master key to success. Technology has not only transformed how we interact with consumers, but has also redefined the very essence of human connection in the business world.

At this point, we bid farewell to the old guard and embrace a dawn full of infinite possibilities. Marketing and sales are no longer just a transaction, but an immersive experience that uses artificial intelligence to understand and anticipate each customer's needs. Adaptation, then, becomes a strategic dance that guides every move toward sustainable success.

So, dear reader, as you close this book, we invite you to take the spark of adaptation with you. Let it be the compass on your journey through the changing landscape of marketing and sales. May this journey have ignited the flame of curiosity and innovation in your mind, and may artificial intelligence be your ally in every step you take.

The power of adaptation is in your hands. Go ahead, challenge the norms, embrace change and build a future where marketing and sales merge in a harmonious symphony of creativity, technology and human connection. May your path be illuminated by the glow of the new dawn that artificial intelligence and adaptation offer you!